RESOURCE BOOKS FOR TEACHERS

*series editor*

ALAN MALEY

# CONVERSATION

Rob Nolasco &
Lois Arthur



Oxford University Press

Oxford University Press
Walton Street, Oxford OX2 6DP

*Oxford New York*
*Athens Auckland Bangkok Bombay*
*Calcutta Cape Town Dar es Salaam Delhi*
*Florence Hong Kong Istanbul Karachi*
*Kuala Lumpur Madras Madrid Melbourne*
*Mexico City Nairobi Paris Singapore*
*Taipei Tokyo Toronto*

and associated companies in
*Berlin Ibadan*

*Oxford* and *Oxford English* are trade marks of Oxford University Press.

ISBN 0 19 437096 8



First published 1987
Seventh impression 1994



Set by Katerprint Typesetting Services, Oxford

Printed in Hong Kong

# Acknowledgements

The publishers would like to thank the following for their permission to use copyright material:

Nathaniel Altman and Thorsons Publishing Group Limited for an extract from *The Palmistry Workbook* (1984); Charles Handy and BBC Publications for an extract from *Taking Stock – Being Fifty in the Eighties* (1983); Donald Norfolk and Michael Joseph Ltd. for an extract from *Farewell to Fatigue* (1985); Oxford University Press for an extract from the *English Language Teaching Journal*, Vol. 40/2 (April 1986); Gordon Wells and Cambridge University Press for an extract from *Learning Through Interaction* (1981).

# Contents

# The authors and series editor

**Rob Nolasco** has been involved in English as a foreign language since 1970. He was part of the senior management of The British Council managed ESP project at King Abdulaziz University, Jeddah (1978–80). Between 1981 and 1983 he was a Project Director with the Overseas Development Administration in Angola, and with The Centre for British Teachers Ltd. in Morocco (1983–85). He has also taught EFL to secondary and adult students, at all levels, in the UK, Turkey, France, and Spain. He is currently working as a freelance teacher-trainer and writer, and EFL consultant. He is the author of several books in the Oxford Supplementary Skills series (OUP) and *Streetwise* (OUP, 1992).

**Lois Arthur** started her career with The Centre for British Teachers Ltd. in West Germany. In 1979 she took up the post of Senior Tutor at The Bell School of Languages at Cambridge. Between 1983 and 1985 she was the Deputy Project Director with The Centre for British Teachers Ltd. in Morocco. She currently works as Trust Courses Manager for The Bell Educational Trust, with specific responsibility for developing junior courses.

**Alan Maley** worked for The British Council from 1962–1988, serving as English Language Officer in Yugoslavia, Ghana, Italy, France, and China, and as Regional Representative for The British Council in South India (Madras). From 1988–1993 he was Director-General of the Bell Educational Trust, Cambridge. He is currently Senior Fellow in the Department of English Language and Literature of the National University of Singapore.

He wrote *Quartet* (with Françoise Grellet and Wim Welsing, OUP 1982). He has also written *Beyond Words*, *Sounds Interesting*, *Sounds Intriguing*, *Words*, *Variations on a Theme*, and *Drama Techniques in Language Learning* (all with Alan Duff), *The Mind's Eye* (with Françoise Grellet and Alan Duff), and *Learning to Listen* and *Poem into Poem* (with Sandra Moulding). He is also Series Editor for the New Perspectives and the Oxford Supplementary Skills series.

# Foreword

The distinction between accuracy and fluency is now a familiar one. Almost as familiar is the further distinction between fluency and appropriacy. To be accurate is not necessarily to be fluent. And to be fluent is not necessarily to be appropriate in a given set of circumstances.

In this book the authors make a further distinction: between speaking skills and conversation skills. They contend that there are skills specific to conversation which make it easier for people to talk to each other informally, and that these do not overlap a hundred per cent with the skills involved in fluent speaking. Being able to speak reasonably correct and even fluent English is one thing. Being able to engage in on-going, interactive, mentally satisfying conversation is another. This is not to deny that speaking skills are necessary for conversation; simply that they are not alone sufficient for successful conversation to take place.

It is these specific conversational skills which the book sets out to cover. In order to do so, the authors first examine in the introduction what it is that native speakers *do* when they 'make conversation'. They then use this information as the basis for the tasks and activities in the remainder of the book.

Two obvious, but nevertheless frequently neglected facts about conversations, are that they involve at least two people, and that the participants in a conversation cannot talk simultaneously all the time. Unless they agree to share the speaking time, listen, react, and attend to each other, the conversation dies.

This is in contrast to a view of speaking, which is often handled as if it were the only factor of importance. Absorption in speaking, without attending to the other, can only lead to surreal parallel monologues, such as we encounter in Pinter. The mutual, interdependent, interactive nature of conversation is given special emphasis in the sections on *Awareness activities* and *Feedback activities*. A series of tasks is developed here to sharpen the students' awareness and observation both of themselves and of others. The importance given to equipping the students with tools to evaluate their own performance (both in the conversations and in their own learning) is especially welcome.

*Conversation* is unique in its insistence on the need to teach conversational skills. The importance it gives to developing a sensitivity to fellow participants in conversations is likewise highly original. Above all it offers a rich and varied selection of activities and tasks to draw upon.

It will be welcomed by all teachers interested in developing further the teaching of this important aspect of oral expression.

Alan Maley

# Introduction

Foreign language teachers often tend to assume that conversation in the language classroom involves nothing more than putting into practice the grammar and vocabulary skills taught elsewhere in the course. So, the 'conversation class' may turn out to include everything from mechanical drills to task-based problem-solving activities. It is true that both these types of activity may, to some extent at least, help students develop the skill of taking part in conversation. But, if we want to teach conversation well, we need to know something about what native speakers do when they have conversations. This information can then help us to develop appropriate materials and techniques for teaching purposes. In this section therefore, we shall be looking at the characteristics of native-speaker conversation in order to provide a rationale for the practical exercises which follow in the remainder of the book.

## What is conversation?

People sometimes use the term 'conversation' to mean any spoken encounter or interaction. In this book however, 'conversation' refers to a time when two or more people have the right to talk or listen without having to follow a fixed schedule, such as an agenda. In conversation everyone can have something to say and anyone can speak at any time. In everyday life we sometimes refer to conversation as 'chat' and the focus of the book is on this type of spoken interaction, rather than on more formal, planned occasions for speaking, such as meetings.

## The functions of conversation

The purposes of conversation include the exchange of information; the creation and maintenance of social relationships such as friendship; the negotiation of status and social roles, as well as deciding on and carrying out joint actions. Conversation therefore has many functions, although its primary purpose in our own language is probably social.

## The units of conversation

The basic unit of conversation is an exchange. An exchange consists of two moves (an initiating move and a response). Each move can also be called a turn, and a turn can be taken without using words, e.g. by a nod of the head. So for this dialogue the move and exchange structure can be illustrated in the following way:

**A** Jane.
**B** Yes?
**A** Could I borrow your bike, please?
**B** Sure, it's in the garage.
**A** Thanks very much.

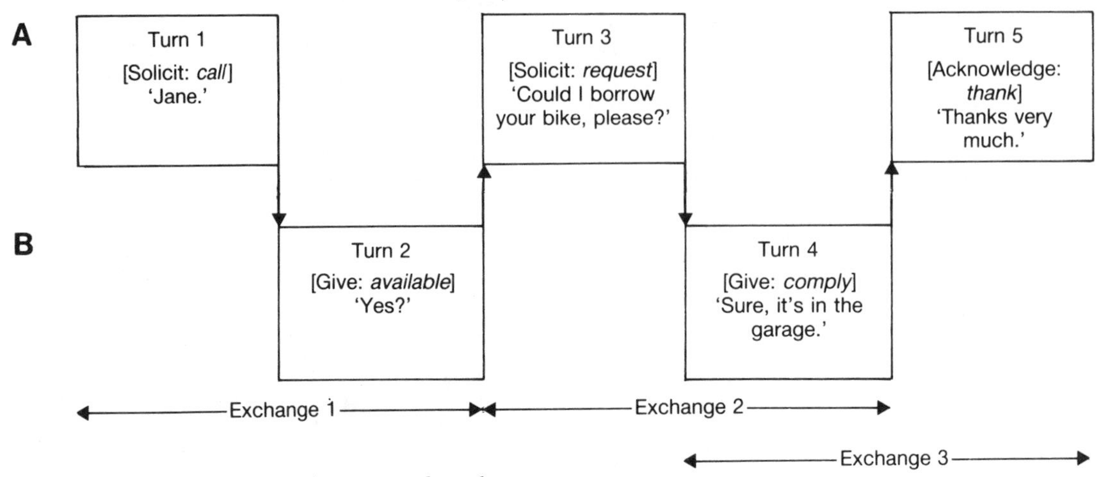


**Figure 1** *An illustration of move and exchange structure*

We can give a function to each move, e.g. request, acknowledge. This may not be easy, and to do so we need to take account of factors such as who the speakers are, where and when the conversation occurs, as well as the position of the move in the stream of speech.

Notice that an exchange, or a series of exchanges, are not necessarily the same thing as a conversation. The following is an example of an exchange:

**A** Hi!
**B** Hi!

The second example contains two exchanges, but it is not a conversation because the two speakers want to finish their business as quickly as possible:

**A** How much are the oranges?
**B** Eighteen pence each, madam.
**A** I'll have two, please.
**B** That's thirty-six pence!

Conversation is open-ended and has the potential to develop in any way. It is possible that the second example could contain a conversation if the speakers decided to talk about the price of oranges. They may do this in order to get a discount, or to develop a social relationship, and the potential is always there in real life. Unfortunately, many students never have the confidence or opportunity to go beyond simple exchanges like the one above, and one of the main objectives of this book is to introduce exercises which allow students to develop the ability to initiate and sustain conversation.

## What do native speakers do in conversation?

Conversation is such a natural part of our lives that many people are not conscious of what happens within it. However, conversation follows certain rules which can be described. For example, when we look at normal conversation we notice that:

- usually only one person speaks at a time;
- the speakers change;
- the length of any contribution varies;
- there are techniques for allowing the other party or parties to speak;
- neither the content nor the amount of what we say is specified in advance.

Conversation analysis seeks to explain how this occurs, and the aim of the sections which follow is to make the readers sensitive to the main issues from a teaching point of view.

## The co-operative principle

Normal conversations proceed so smoothly because we co-operate in them. Grice (1975) has described four maxims or principles which develop co-operative behaviour. These are:

**The maxim of quality**
Make your contribution one that is true. Specifically:
**a.** Do not say what you believe to be false.
**b.** Do not say anything for which you lack adequate evidence.

**The maxim of quantity**
Make your contribution just as informative as required and no more.

**The maxim of relation**
Make your contribution relevant and timely.

**The maxim of manner**
Avoid obscurity and ambiguity.

Readers will realize that these maxims are often broken and, when this happens, native speakers work harder to get at the underlying meaning, e.g.

**A** How did you find the play?
**B** The lighting was good.

By choosing not to be as informative as required, B is probably suggesting the play is not worth commenting on. A lot of the material written for teaching English as a foreign language is deliberately free of such ambiguity. This means that students have problems later in conversational situations where the maxims are not observed. Systematic listening practice using authentic discourse may be one solution.

These maxims may also be observed differently in different cultures, so we need to tell students if they are saying too much or too little without realizing it.

## The making of meaning

When we speak we make promises, give advice or praise, issue threats, etc. Some linguists refer to individual moves as speech acts. Each of the following are examples of speech acts and we can try to allocate a specific function to each example:

- *Turn left at the next street.* (Instruction?)
- *Invest in Crescent Life.* (Advice?)
- *Keep off the grass.* (Order?)

However, we need to know the context of the example to give it a function with any certainty, and it is easy to think of situations in which the examples above might have a different function from the one shown. In conversations the relationship between the speaker and the listener will have an important effect on how the listener understands the particular speech act. For example, the way in which we hear and respond to a statement such as *I've lost my wallet*, may well depend on whether we think the person is trying to obtain money under false pretences or not! There is no room to enter into a full discussion of discourse analysis, but the following issues are particularly relevant to the teaching of conversation.

Most speech acts have more than one function, e.g. when we say to a waitress, *The music is rather loud*, we are simultaneously reporting that we cannot hear ourselves speak, and also complaining and asking the waitress to do something about it. Any approach that leads students to equate one particular language form with one particular language function, will lead to misunderstandings in conversation because an important requirement for success is being able to interpret intended speech acts correctly. There is also a need to help students begin to become sensitive to why a speaker chose a particular speech act, e.g. by setting a listening task which asks students to comment on the purpose of what they hear – is it meant as a challenge, a defence? etc.

## Adjacency

The two moves in an exchange are related to each other through the use of adjacency pairs. These are utterances produced by two successive speakers in which the second utterance can be identified as being related to the first. Some examples of adjacency pairs are:

**1 A** Hello! (Greeting-Greeting)
**B** Hi!

**2 A** Dinner's ready! (Call-Answer)
**B** Coming.

**3 A** Is this yours? (Question-Answer)
**B** No.

In some cases we can predict the second part of a pair from the first. As in example 1, a greeting is normally followed by a greeting. In other cases there are a variety of options. For example, a complaint might be followed by an apology or a justification. Teachers need to think about ways of developing appropriate second parts to adjacency pairs from the start. For example, many drills require students to reply to yes/no questions with 'yes' or 'no', plus a repetition of the verb. We therefore get exchanges like:

**A** Are these cakes fresh?
**B** Yes, they are.

What students do not often get are opportunities to practise other options, such as:

**A** Are these cakes fresh?
**B** I bought them this morning. Help yourself.

Even worse is the tendency to encourage students to produce isolated sentences containing a target structure, e.g. *If I had £10,000 I'd buy a car.* Unless we get away from question-answer-question-answer sequences and the production of sentences without either stimulus or response, students will always appear to be flat and unresponsive in conversation because a minimal answer does nothing to drive the conversation forward. We shall look at how this might be done through controlled activities in Chapter 2.

## Turn taking

As native speakers we find it relatively easy and natural to know who is to speak, when, and for how long. But this skill is not automatically transferred to a foreign language. Many students have great difficulty in getting into a conversation, knowing when to give up their turn to others, and in bringing a conversation to a close. In order for conversation to work smoothly, all participants have to be alert to signals that a speaker is about to finish his or her turn, and be able to come in with a contribution which fits the direction in which the conversation is moving. We need to train students to sense when someone is about to finish. Falling intonation is often a signal for this.

It would also be useful for students to realize that questions like, *Did anyone watch the football last night?* function as a general invitation to someone to develop a conversation. Foreigners also sometimes lose their turn because they hesitate in order to find the right word. Teaching our students expressions like, *Wait, there's more*, or *That's not all*, as well as fillers and hesitation devices such as *Erm . . ., Well . . ., so you can guess what happened . . .*, etc. will help them to keep going. Finally, it is well worth looking at ways in which we initiate and build on what others have said such as *That's like what happened to me . . .* and *Did I tell you about when . . .?*, so that students can make appropriate contributions. Some relevant activities can be found in Chapters 3 and 5.

# Openings and closings

The devices used for opening and closing different conversations are very similar. Many conversations start with adjacency pairs designed to attract attention, such as:

1 **A** Have you got a light?
  **B** Sure.

2 **A** Gosh it's hot in here today.
  **B** I'm used to it.

Openings such as these allow further talk once the other person's attention has been obtained. Many foreign students use openings that make them sound too direct and intrusive, for example, by asking a very direct question. Closing too presents a problem when the sudden introduction of a final move like, *Goodbye* makes the foreigner sound rude. Native speakers will tend to negotiate the end of a conversation so that nobody is left talking, and you will hear expressions like:

- *OK then . . .*
- *Right . . .*
- *Well, I suppose . . .*
- *Erm, I'm afraid . . .*
- *I've got to go now.*
- *I'll let you get back to your writing.*
- *So I'll see you next week.*

It is worth pointing these out. Native speakers sometimes try to cut a conversation short by only producing a minimal response or even saying nothing at all, but neither strategy is recommended for students of English.

# Topics

Different cultures talk about different things in their everyday lives. Native speakers are very aware of what they should and should not talk about with specific categories of people in their own language, but the rules may be different in a foreign language. Both teachers and students need to develop a sense of 'taboo' subjects if they are to avoid offence.

# Male and female differences in conversation

Current research reveals interesting sex differences in conversation among native speakers. Women, for example, are more likely to show an interest in personal details than men. They are also better listeners and more likely to help the person they are speaking to develop a topic, by asking information questions and making encouraging remarks and gestures. However, men are more reluctant to disclose personal information. They prefer it when there is a purpose for the conversation and they would rather talk about outside topics, e.g. games, hobbies, politics, cars, etc. than themselves. This may influence our choice of topic.

# Simplification in informal speech

There are many foreign students who pronounce the individual sounds and words of English beautifully but who still sound very foreign. The reason is that in English the sound quality of a word, particularly the vowels and certain consonants, changes depending on whether the word is said in isolation or as part of a continuous stream of words. Some of this is a result of simplification of informal speech. One important reason for simplification is that English is a stress-timed language. When we speak, all the stressed syllables in our sentences tend to come at roughly similar intervals of time. This means that the following sentences (taken from Broughton *et al* 1978), when spoken by the same speaker in normal circumstances, would take the same amount of time to say, even though they contain different numbers of words or syllables.

**1** I *bought* a *dog*.
**2** It's a *dog* I *bought*.
**3** But it's a *dog* that I *bought*.

They are the same length when spoken because they contain the same number of stressed syllables (*dog* and *bought*). This means that the unstressed syllables have to be squeezed in and the vowels, which are in unstressed syllables, very often become the neutral or weak vowel, or 'schwa' which is represented by the symbol [ə]. This is the most common sound in spoken English and the use of weak forms means a native speaker will tend to say:

- *It was him.* /ɪt wəz hɪm/ not /ɪt wɒz hɪm/
- *Give it to me.* /gɪv ɪt tə mi/ not /gɪv ɪt tu: mi/

Elision, which is the 'missing out' of a consonant or vowel, or both, is also very common. A native speaker would tend to say:

/'fɜ:s'θri:/ not /'fɜ:st'θri:/ for 'first three'.

For foreigners (particularly those whose native language is syllabus-timed, e.g. French), the tendency is to give each part of a word the same value and this can have a wearying effect on the native speaker listener, who will, as a result, be less likely to remain sympathetic and interested. It is therefore worth pointing out weak forms from the start for recognition and production.

## Stress and intonation

Good conversationalists use stress and intonation to keep conversations going. A fall on words like 'OK' or 'So', often serves to show that we are about to change the subject. A rise on 'really' is a way of showing interest. All of these are important signals and it is worth pointing these out to students when they occur so that they start listening for them. A wide voice range is also more likely to keep a listener interested than a monotone. This can be difficult for students whose native language has a narrow voice range, and for these students additional sensitivity training may be needed. Students also need to realize that the wrong intonation can lead to misunderstanding. For example, researchers found that Pakistani ladies who were serving in the canteen of Heathrow often got a hostile reaction by pronouncing the word 'gravy' with a falling intonation, rather than the rise which would be polite in British English.

## Gesture and body language

While it is true that speakers of English do not use as much gesture as people in some other cultures, e.g. Italians, they do use their hands to emphasize a point. The positioning of the body also has an effect on the listener. Sitting on the edge of a seat may be seen as being aggressive. Slumping in it is a sign of boredom, and even where we do not mean it this may be how it comes across. In some cultures people also stand very close to those they are talking to and many Americans report discomfort when faced with Middle-Easterners who tend to value proximity and touch. Body language is a complicated area but it is worth observing your students and giving them feedback on how they appear to others.

# Summary

Teachers need to be aware of the characteristics of native-speaker performance in conversation if they are to teach conversation effectively. They also need to consider which of the functions of conversation are most relevant to the students. These will vary according to level and needs, but most general purpose students would want to use English to

- give and receive information;
- collaborate in doing something;
- share personal experiences and opinions with a view to building social relationships.

Students will not be able to do these things by talking *about* conversation, and the stress in this book is *learning by doing* through activities which give students practice in a pattern of interaction that is as close as possible to what competent native speakers do in real life. This is the purpose of the *Fluency activities* in Chapter 4. However we recognize that students need guidance and support in the early stages and this is the rationale behind the *Controlled activities* in Chapter 2. We also believe that the performance of the students can be improved by increasing their sensitivity to the way that conversation works, and the tasks in Chapter 3 are mostly aimed at developing awareness. The other vital ingredient is feedback. Students need to be able to assess their progress so that it is possible to identify areas for further practice, and this issue is treated in Chapter 5.

Finally, the key to the smooth operation of task-based fluency work is the effective management of the materials, of the students, and of the classroom environment. The cry from many students 'I just want conversation lessons', or 'I just want to practise talking; I know the grammar', suggests that conversation lessons are somehow easier to prepare and teach, are inferior in status to 'the grammar lesson', and so on. Yet many teachers will know to their cost how often the conversation lesson just does not quite work. In Chapter 1 we look at how the activities in the book can be used and put together to provide a coherent and purposeful approach. Above all we hope that users of the book will find the approach suggested practical, useful, and interesting enough to develop ideas along similar lines.

# 1 Towards a classroom approach

## Introduction

The purpose of this chapter is to give a brief account of how the activities which can be found in chapters 2 to 5 can be combined to provide a coherent approach to the teaching of conversation. Although many students say that their main purpose in learning English is to be able to speak it, many students will not talk readily in class, and the 'discussion lesson' in which the teacher does most of the talking is still too prevalent. If you find that this is happening consistently then you should pause and ask yourself the following questions:

**1** Do I make an effort to prepare students for the discussion or fluency activity?

Preparation is a vital ingredient for success. Students need to be orientated to the topic, and an instruction like 'Let's talk about euthanasia' rarely works. Some of the fluency tasks in Chapter 4 have pre-tasks built in but some students may need more orientation to a topic than others for cultural or linguistic reasons. Some simple techniques which can be used to prepare students for a particular topic include:

- The use of audio/visual aids to arouse interest.
- A general orientation to the topic by means of a short text, questionnaire, series of statements for discussion and modification, a video extract, etc. The only rule is that the pre-task should never be too long.
- Exercises to build up the vocabulary needed for a task. This can include matching words to pictures, putting words from a list into different categories, learning words from lists, etc.

**2** Do students know what is expected of them?

Students may need to be orientated to the task itself so that they know what is expected of them. For example, the instruction to 'discuss' a topic may be meaningless to many students who do not come from a culture where such discussion is a normal part of the educational process. In some cases students may need training, and this is discussed briefly later in this chapter. The general rule is to formulate tasks in terms students can understand and make sure that the instructions are clear. In giving instructions we should always:

- Think through instructions from the point of view of the student.
- Stage the instructions carefully and make sure the students understand at each stage. Do this by asking for a demonstration or for an answer to a question which proves understanding. A 'yes/no' answer to *Do you understand?* is not particularly revealing. If the task is very complex it might be advisable to set up a rehearsal before asking students to start.
- Make sure that instructions are given clearly. Insist on silence and make sure you can be seen. Use demonstration and gestures where possible.

**3** Have I made an effort to find out which topics will motivate students to speak?

Students are sometimes not motivated to talk because they lack involvement in the topic. However, even where students admit interest, they may be reluctant or unwilling to talk about it in English because they lack the linguistic resources to give a subject the treatment it deserves. This would certainly be true of issues like 'euthanasia'. As teachers we should also remember that it is not always natural to enter into prolonged discussion on controversial topics. More often than not we limit ourselves to strong opinion rather than extended and reasoned argument. As native speakers we tend to talk about things which are within our experience, and tasks built around the following sorts of areas usually generate a lot of discussion when they are used with adult students:

| | |
|---|---|
| family life | money |
| sport | personal experiences |
| change | dreams |
| holidays | food |
| pleasures | health |

Always check by asking students what they thought about the topic at the end of the lesson.

**4** Is there any follow-up to the discussion?

Adult students will always be reluctant to take part in a discussion if they feel it has no educational value. A clear explanation of the rationale of the tasks, as well as the use of feedback tasks or report back sessions (see Chapter 5), are important ways of counteracting this. In short a successful conversation programme involves a lot more than a vague commitment to talk about something. The questions we have looked at refer to central management issues. We can now see how the tasks in this book can be put together to form a programme.

# Classes of activity

There are four basic types of activities in this book:

- Controlled activities to give students confidence and support. (Chapter 2)
- Awareness activities to increase sensitivity in students to what they are aiming at. (Chapter 3)
- Fluency activities to give students the practice they need to *use* English for communication. (Chapter 4)
- Feedback tasks to allow students to reflect on their own performance so that they become aware of areas in which they have to improve. (Chapter 5)

In most conversation programmes we would expect a mixture of all of these activities from the start, geared to the needs of the students. When we think about the mix, the following considerations apply:

**1** It may be necessary to introduce fluency activities gradually. Students who are used to highly controlled patterns of interaction, where it is the teacher who initiates all the language exchanges and judges whether they are correct or not, may find that fluency activities pose a considerable threat because they are not used to the freedom involved. In these cases we would need to introduce students gradually to freer activities as the timetable (on the next page) from an article in *English Language Teaching Journal* indicates.

Obviously students will vary in terms of their prior learning experience, so it is always worth seeing what they are used to because they may need a period of adjustment to new ways of working. Remember too that we are talking about a continuous process. Students who are used to pair and group work may need to be introduced to project work, for instance. Having said this, if students are confident and not threatened there is no reason why fluency-type activities should not be used from the earliest stages.

**2** It is also unlikely that any one lesson will consist entirely of one type of activity. It is always best to aim for variety of task type.

**3** Different types of activities will be used in different proportions according to the level. For example, advanced students will need relatively few controlled activities and the narrow focus of these tasks would be replaced by awareness tasks. For beginners the situation is reversed and while it is always worth pointing out features such as hesitation devices, full-blown awareness tasks would be the exception rather than the rule, and there would tend to be a higher proportion of controlled activities.

*Table 1: A ten-week plan for introducing students to and training them in the use of pair and group work*[3]

| Week | Aim | Means |
|---|---|---|
| 1 | To extend responsibility for initiating short responses to the learner. | Teacher-controlled open and adjacent pair work on question-and-answer exercises. |
| 2 | Consolidation plus introduction of dialogue exchange in pairs. | Dialogue reading: learner takes one part. Move from Teacher reading A and learners B through open and adjacent pairs to whole class work in closed pairs. |
| 3 | Consolidation plus introduction of learners to the habit of choosing the content of communication in oral work. | Longer read dialogues, followed by the introduction of cued dialogues. |
| 4 | Consolidation plus introduction of the idea of working together in English. | Introduce discourse chains to prompt recall of known dialogues; get learners to work on comprehension exercises in English. |
| 5 | To introduce the idea of guided role play, as well as simple problem solving. | Introduce role cards on the basis of familiar material; a short period in closed pairs; work on problems of grammar. |
| 6 | Consolidation plus introduction of 'information-gap' exercises. | Longer guided role plays; practice in moving quickly into pair work exercises; information gap in which half the class sees the picture; teacher controls questions and answers. |
| 7 | Consolidation and extension. | Information gap similar to (6), but done in closed pairs; jigsaw reading. |
| 8 | Consolidation and extension. | Introduce free role-play activities in pairs, then threes and fours; small group essay preparation for the final stage of guided composition lesson. |
| 9 | Consolidation and extension. | Introduce ranking activities. |
| 10 | Consolidation and extension. | Group preparation of ideas and structure for essay. |

# Achieving a balanced programme

The amount of time available for conversation work will obviously depend on the intensity of the programme as well as its emphasis. As the amount of contact time available varies considerably, the aim is to give general advice which will need to be interpreted locally. If a group meets for one and a half hours a week, then it is conceivable that conversational competence would be its sole objective. In this situation it is recommended that students get a balance of the four different types of activities mentioned in the previous section each time they meet the teacher. Obviously the proportion of time spent on activities will vary according to the level of the students, their prior knowledge, etc. but an intermediate group might do the following within the time available. The 'Dialogue fill-in' activity (Chapter 2 page 41) would be completed as a preparation for one of the activities which involve the sharing of personal information, e.g. 'Emotional match' (Chapter 4 page 90). This might in turn be followed by an abbreviated version of a Feedback task (Chapter 5 pages 126/7). Clearly the range of options is infinite, and the awareness/controlled activity does not have to be related to the fluency activity for that week. This allows for recycling and building. It would however always be wise to point out the aim of the activities at all stages.

Students who are following a full time language programme can obviously spend a lot more time on conversational work, but the kind of mix outlined above applies just as well, although it may be possible to spend a little more time on each activity. In their case preparation and remedial work can and should be a part of the teaching of grammar and a lot of the work on areas such as conversational gambits, pronunciation, rhythm, stress and intonation, can be integrated into the wider programme. On the whole the aim should be for 'little and often' rather than long sessions devoted entirely to one particular area.

# Persuading the learner

As we have said, student-resistance is a problem teachers encounter. The most likely cause is unfamiliarity with the way in which a programme is organized. The solution is to tell them *why*. In our experience, appeals to common sense work far better than self-justificatory argument or discussion, and it is important to find a way of presenting a clear and simple rationale of the approach from the outset. This may simply be a quick outline of the nature of the different types of activities used and their relationship to each other. It may also be appropriate to point out the way in which the activities serve to meet the students' objectives. In this way students will perceive that the programme has purpose and direction.

Students may also need information on *how* to go about the activities. This information may take the form of:

- A staged and gradual introduction for students from very traditional backgrounds.
- A demonstration or discussion of what is expected of them. Many students, for example, may not be familiar with the role of an observer and may need to be shown what to do.
- Advice or discussion on how to make the most of the opportunities available when working in a student-centred context. For example, some students do not give peer group work the same status as sessions in which the teacher is up front. They may therefore miss opportunities to get down new words and expressions because they feel these can only come from the teacher.
- Instructions on how to get started quickly, how to use the equipment, etc.

Some students may never have been asked to work independently of the teacher in a classroom setting before. To help this situation some useful pre-course work could include orientation talks by more advanced students from a similar socio-cultural background, as well as a discussion of films or photographs of students taking part in group work, projects, etc. Analysing *how* activities were performed should also be an object of discussion in general course feedback sessions, as this would provide useful information on how the students perceive the course.

## A sense of progress

The emphasis on recording and feedback tasks of the sort outlined in Chapter 5 is important in ensuring that students develop a sense that they are making progress. Often students do not realize just how much more confident and fluent they are becoming. One reason may be that as they improve, the listener makes fewer concessions and, as conversation is a two way process, students do not feel they are making progress because they may understand less and therefore not be in a position to respond. This is particularly true for students studying in an environment where English is spoken. A sense of not improving may also arise because students may rarely get the opportunity to take a leading role in conversation, and it is well worth trying to programme sessions in which advanced or upper intermediate students have to sustain a conversation with those at a lower level, in order to give them the experience of being the driving force in a conversation. Getting students to compare their current efforts with recordings made in the earliest stages of the course is another way of boosting confidence.

In many cases students will have external objectives such as the oral examinations run by organizations such as ARELS, the RSA, and The University of Cambridge Local Examinations Syndicate. It is therefore useful to show the extent to which students are making progress towards their examination objective by including an element of exam practice in the programme. There are a variety of ways in which this can be set up but the following represents a possible approach.

- Make the students fully aware of what a satisfactory performance in the examination involves. For example, a film of a First Certificate interview might be used in conjunction with a version of the activities on pages 54/5 and 126/7, to show students how interviewers tend to use a signal like, *How interesting*, to encourage students to say more.
- An identification of areas which are critical for a good performance in the exam might then be followed by controlled practice of exam-type tasks.
- Students should also be given practice in exam conditions. Feedback from these tasks is particularly valuable in that it fosters self-evaluation and improvement.

There is no room to give assessment of conversation the treatment it deserves. There may be a need to give students a grade for the work they do in the conversation lessons and, as continuous assessment is particularly suited to assessing conversational performance, there is a need to keep good records. Whether the results are expressed in terms of letter grades or numbers may be a matter of preference or the dictates of the system. There is however an interest in being able to describe the students' performance in behavioural terms and teachers are encouraged to look at the scales developed by The British Council, or the Foreign Service Institute to see if the scales can be adapted to their purposes. *Testing Communicative Performance* by Brendan Carroll (1982), is a summary of the early work done by The British Council's Testing Service, and more recent information may be available from the English Language Testing Service, The British Council, 10 Spring Gardens, London SW1A 2BN.

# 2 Controlled activities

## Introduction

Although conversational competence can only come from fluency activities or natural language interaction outside the classroom, there is an argument for the use of controlled activities which help students develop confidence as well as the ability to participate in and maintain simple, commonly encountered conversations.

Many students have to overcome a psychological barrier before they are prepared to speak in the foreign language. Some students find speaking in the classroom situation a threat because there is always an audience, and consequently prefer the anonymity of one-to-one encounters outside. Others on the other hand who quite happily contribute in the sheltered environment of the classroom, experience considerable problems in building up the courage to use the language outside class. A few prefer not to speak at all, and are consequently denied opportunities for practice. Within the classroom a major source of threat is the individual's perception of himself or herself and the other students. Threat reduction is possible by building up personal security through the use of 'getting to know you' activities which promote trust, as well as 'articulation' activities which give students the opportunity to use English sounds in a safe and undemanding environment.

The other main group of activities in this chapter aim to help students develop their ability to take part in sustained conversation through activities which give controlled practice in the building blocks of conversation using dialogue building techniques such as cloze dialogues, by paying attention to exchange structure, and the short responses known as gambits, as well as through grammar practice.

## Getting-to-know-you activities

Students are a lot happier to speak or make mistakes if there is a positive atmosphere of trust within a group. This is unlikely to develop quickly unless the group begins by getting to know each other's names. Activities which serve to promote exchange of personal information also promote trust and confidence. The following selection of activities are designed to do this.

# 1 Chain names

**LEVEL**

**Any level** (including beginners)

**TIME**

**5–10 minutes**

**AIM**

To introduce students to each other.

**PREPARATION**

None.

**PROCEDURE**

**1** Ask the students to sit in a semi-circle, and nominate one student to introduce himself or herself.

**2** The person next to him or her must then repeat his or her name, and then introduce himself or herself.

**3** Ask your students to repeat this procedure around the semi-circle, each one repeating the name of the person before them, and then saying their own name. For example:

**A** I'm Rob.
**B** Rob, I'm Paula.
**C** Rob, Paula, I'm Francisco.
**D** Rob, Paula, Francisco, I'm Dieter.

More advanced students might tackle the following:

**A** I'm Francisco, I'm from Bilbao.
**B** He's Francisco. He's from Bilbao. I'm Bianca, and I'm from Rome.
**C** He's Francisco. He's from Bilbao. She's Bianca. She's from Rome. I'm Pierre, and I'm from Toulouse.

**REMARKS**

**1** Twelve represents a maximum number for this activity.

**2** You should always take a turn to show you are learning too.

# 2 Name bingo

**LEVEL**

**Beginner to Elementary**

**TIME**

**10–15 minutes**

**AIM**

To introduce students to each other (particularly suitable for large classes).

**PREPARATION**

Prepare a blank seating plan of the class, and make enough photocopies for the whole class.

**PROCEDURE**

**1** Start by practising name learning in the usual way, e.g. *Hello, my name's Carla, what's your name?*

**2** Then tell the students that they must remember as many names as possible during the next practice phase.

**3** Continue the practice, making sure you ask every student at least once.

**4** Give out a blank seating plan of the class to each student and ask them to complete it with as many names as they can remember (this should take four to five minutes, and cheating is not serious as long as it is not disruptive).

**5** The object of the next stage is for one student in the class to name all the others with the aid of his or her plan, and using, *His name's . . .*, *Her name's . . . .* Ask a student who feels he or she has most or all of the names to start. As soon as he or she makes a mistake he or she has to sit down and either you nominate another student or someone volunteers.

**6** Tell the students that they may add names to their plans during this phase.

**7** The winner is the student who gets through the whole class without a mistake. As the game progresses more and more students should feel able to name everyone. The game can continue as long as the students are motivated. They can also try to name everyone without the help of the plan.

**8** Take a turn in the middle yourself to motivate the more reticent students.

**REMARKS**

**1** Many of the suggestions for name learning games involve small group interaction and cannot be used in a secondary school environment with fixed desks, etc. 'Name bingo' can be used with large classes, but it can also be used with smaller classes if students are asked to work from memory after the initial stages.

**2** For further examples see *Grammar in Action* by Mario Rinvolucri and Christine Frank, (1983), and *Teaching Techniques for Communicative English* by Jane Revell, (1979).

## 3 Find someone who

**LEVEL**

**Elementary and above**

**TIME**

**15–20 minutes**

**AIM**

To enable students to find out more about each other.

**PREPARATION**

Prepare task sheets for the students to complete, like the one over the page. Go through your students' application forms, initial interview notes, etc. to get an interesting piece of information about each of your students to incorporate into the task sheets.

| Find someone in the class who: | Name |
|---|---|
| 1 plays the piano | ................ |
| 2 is training to be a doctor | ................ |
| 3 was born in Australia | ................ |
| etc. | |

**PROCEDURE**

1 Give out a task sheet to each student and give them about 10 minutes to try and complete it. Encourage them to mill around.

2 When the buzz begins to subside call the students together and go through the task sheets by asking questions like, *Who plays the piano? Who was born in Australia?* etc. Allow any of the students to answer.

**REMARKS**

An activity like 'Find someone who' is best used very early on in the course. Consequently students may be reluctant to move around if they are not used to doing this. Encourage them if necessary. There are a number of published versions of this activity, but these are not sensitive to individuals in the group, and therefore do not necessarily perform the introductory function as well. Although this activity is linguistically very simple, it has been used successfully at all levels.

**Acknowledgement**
We first encountered a version of this activity at a workshop run by Gertrude Moskowitz at TESOL, Detroit.

## 4 Guess who?

**LEVEL**

**Elementary to Intermediate**

**TIME**

**15–20 minutes**

**AIM**

Students are given statements of personal information about other students and they have to ask questions in order to establish the person's identity.

**PREPARATION**

Have available enough small pieces of paper for the whole class.

**PROCEDURE**

1 Give each of your students a piece of paper and ask them to write four facts about themselves. These can be anything they choose, e.g. *I was born in February, I own a bicycle, I like Beethoven,* etc. as long as the statement is true.

**2** Tell the students to fold their pieces of paper and pass them anonymously to the front of the class.

**3** Collect them together and then redistribute them so that each student has personal information about another student.

**4** Once the students have had a chance to look at the personal information, tell them that they will have to find out whose information they have by turning the statements into questions, and then asking other students those questions. You can exercise control over the activity in a variety of ways:

- By deciding on the form of question which is allowable, i.e. open questions to the class, such as *Who was born in February?* or questions to individuals, such as *Were you born in February?*
- By deciding whether to nominate students to speak, or to allow them free choice.
- By deciding whether or not to allow the students to move about.

**5** Once you have decided on the rules for the activity you can set it in motion. The activity ends when everybody has found out whose personal information they have.

**REMARKS**

If the initial statements were collected in the previous lesson, or copied out two or three times, you could distribute more than one set of information to each student. This would be needed to make a mingling activity more successful.

# Articulation activities

When students come to speak in a foreign language they often find themselves inhibited by the prospect of having to make what to them are strange and even comic sounds. In severe cases students can become so tongue-tied that they refuse to speak at all. One way of alleviating this problem is to give students the opportunity to experiment with sounds, as well as talk in a secure environment from the start. Often this involves allowing them to experiment individually or in a relaxed group situation.

## 5 Sounds English

**LEVEL**

**Any level**

**TIME**

**10–15 minutes**

**AIM**

An imitation exercise to get students used to getting their tongues round English sounds.

**PREPARATION**

Make a list of items for practice. These could include individual sounds such as the vowels (a-e-i-o-u), as well as short utterances such as *What?*, *You're where?*, *A big black book*, etc.

**PROCEDURE**

1 Explain to the students that they are going to have some fun so as to 'sound English'. (Explain the rationale if necessary.)

2 All of this has to be conducted with a light touch and you should be seen to be making a fool of yourself, too.

3 You should practice the vowels and short utterances, stretching them to their limits of acceptability in English, because the essential thing to do is to exaggerate. Students who do not usually go quite as far as they need to will be trying to imitate you and 'sound English'.

4 Walk around the class correcting the students and give them a chance to rehearse in pairs, if necessary.

**REMARKS**

Making a joke of a real problem releases tension and prepares the students to exaggerate sufficiently to sound English. This is not however, an activity to try with a class who have not had a chance to get to know each other a little. It is also not suitable for large classes.

**Acknowledgement**
We learnt this activity from Tim Johns.

## 6 Look and speak

**LEVEL**

**Beginner to Intermediate**

**TIME**

**15–20 minutes**

**AIM**

To help students repeat a dialogue they have been studying in a natural way.

**PREPARATION**

None.

**PROCEDURE**

1 Divide your students into groups of three with one person acting as a prompter at any stage of the activity.

2 If the dialogue is a short one you can give the participants a few minutes to try and learn it by heart.

3 After that ask two of the students to close their books and try to repeat the dialogue as best they can. The prompter's role is to help them.

4 If the dialogue is longer tell the student who is to start to take in as much of a line as possible, and then making eye contact with the other 'speaker', ask him or her to deliver the line.

5 Continue this with each of the 'speakers' taking a line of dialogue until the reading is complete.

6 Ask the students to go through a dialogue three times exchanging roles each time. This technique gives a simple practice without the disastrous effect of a reading.

**Acknowledgement**
This activity comes from an idea by G Tunnell in *Modern English Teacher* Vol II Number I, 1983.

## 7 Listen and speak

**LEVEL**
**Beginner to Elementary**

**TIME**
**15–20 minutes**

**AIM**
To give students the chance to get simple oral practice by repeating a dialogue they hear for the first time.

**PREPARATION**
None by the teacher. Self-directed.

**PROCEDURE**
1 Divide the students into groups of three and ask them to sit around a cassette/tape recorder.

2 Ask them to select a piece of listening material from a coursebook they are using. Ideally they should not have gone through the dialogue in class, but weaker students may prefer this.

3 Ask one student to act as the prompter who is allowed to consult the tapescript, if necessary.

4 The other two students take a part each and try to repeat what they hear on the tape. Tell them that they should start by doing this on a line-by-line basis and try to progress through to repeating the whole dialogue. Having got the form, they should concentrate on rhythm, intonation and pronunciation.

**REMARKS**
This technique was used with some success with beginners in Angola. There was no language laboratory available but the more social nature of the task seemed to appeal, and the quality of repetition was higher than that encountered in a lab. Students also derive great benefit from using their ears rather than their eyes, and the prompter stops them from cheating.

## 8 Listen and record

**LEVEL**
**Elementary and above**

**TIME**
**15–20 minutes**

**AIM**
For students to make a recording after listening carefully to a taped model.

**PREPARATION**
Select a natural model for students to imitate.

**PROCEDURE**

Ask the students to listen to the tape and to repeat any of the utterances they have heard, until they are ready to be recorded. The activity is self-directed, but you should be available for consultation. The finished product can be a subject of feedback and evaluation.

**REMARKS**

The activity is self-regulatory. This is important if students are not to be threatened by having to repeat something they feel uncertain about. This activity also fosters the notion of rehearsing what we are about to say, something many people do in their own language, anyway.

## 9 Shadow reading

**LEVEL**

**Any level**

**TIME**

**10–15 minutes,** depending on the length of the passage.

**AIM**

To build up students' confidence.

**PREPARATION**

Prepare a suitable master tape of dialogue or text being read aloud, for use in a language laboratory.

**PROCEDURE**

1 Ask your students to listen to the master track once or twice.

2 Once they are ready the objective is to maintain the same rhythm, intonation, stress and pronunciation as the original by repeating *with* the master track.

3 Make sure the students work with the same tape until they are ready to record their own version, or they can ask you to listen to them.

**REMARKS**

The advantage of this use of a language laboratory is that it is a safe and undemanding environment where students can work privately at their own pace.

# Dialogue building

The use of cues or prompts to build up dialogues has become a favoured technique in recent years. The cues or prompts serve to determine the content of what is said, and dialogue building activities can range from being highly controlled to very free. Dialogue building is not a substitute for fluency work, but used sparingly it allows the possibility of giving weaker students a chance to say something. It can also allow teachers to focus on appropriacy so that students get a chance to widen their repertoire. Here are examples of just a few of the types of activities available.

# 10 Who do you think . . .?

**LEVEL**
**Upper intermediate to Advanced**

**TIME**
**20–25 minutes**

**AIM**
To highlight how the same interactional work can be carried out using different language.

**PREPARATION**
Prepare some instructions for your students (A and B) on a task sheet or on separate cards (see below), and make enough photocopies for half the class. Make photocopies of the flow chart over the page.

**PROCEDURE**
**1** Divide your students into pairs. Explain how a discourse chain works. (A discourse chain is used to prompt a dialogue. Individual responses can vary but they should serve the same function within the frame of the given conversation.) Make sure your students understand this before giving out the task sheets.

**2** Set the task in context and ask the students to take a role each.

**3** Ideally students should make a recording which can be played to the rest of the class. If tape recorders are not available, some of the pairs could perform the dialogue. Get the class to listen critically to each version so as to focus on the appropriacy of the different choices.

**4** You can substitute 'language school' in the task sheet for any organization or field of activity your students are familiar with.

---

**TASK SHEET**
Read this introduction:

A and B are colleagues in a language school and they meet in the corridor. A has heard a strong rumour that the Director, Peter West, who is retiring, is going to be replaced by John Stevens. John Stevens was until recently the Director of a rival organization, and A wants to discuss this. B has been given this information confidentially and wants to avoid the subject.

Now go on with the task:

Decide on which role each of you is going to take. Now read through the following model and try to understand your part in the conversation. You have five minutes to prepare what you might say. When you are ready start recording. Review the tape when you have finished and try to correct any expressions which sound inappropriate. Try again as many times as you want, but be ready to play your final tape to the whole class.

---

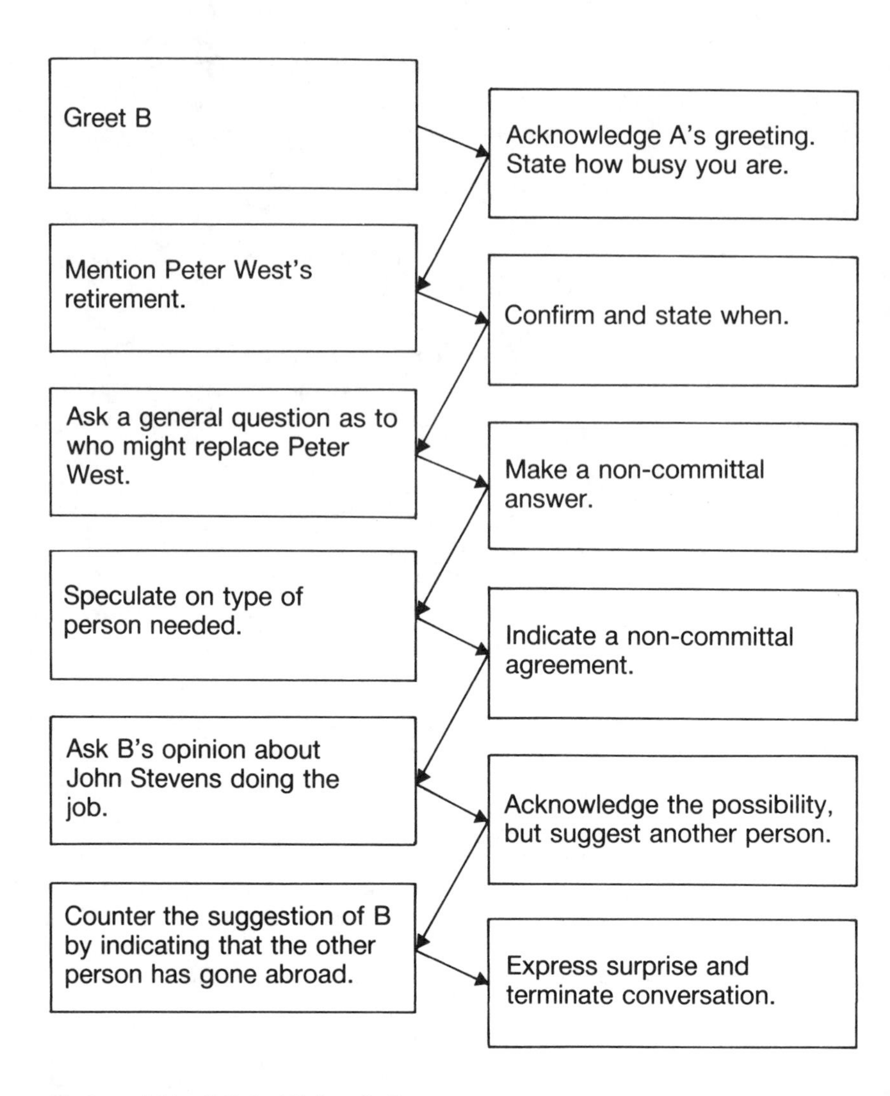




# 11 Do you come here often?

**LEVEL** — **Elementary and above**

**TIME** — **10–15 minutes**

**AIM** — To provide controlled practice where students have to listen very carefully to what the other speaker says.

**PREPARATION** — Prepare a set of cue cards for each of the students (see examples opposite).

**PROCEDURE** — **1** Divide your students into pairs. Give each student one part of a conversation on a card. Each part has a series of options.

**2** Ask the students to listen very carefully to what their partner says in order to give an appropriate response chosen from the options on their card.

**3** Encourage them to go through the options once or twice before swopping cards. End this part of the lesson by getting some of the pairs to demonstrate.

### CUE CARD A

You are by the swimming pool of an exclusive club. You start the conversation:

**A** Do you come here often?
**B** . . .

Now choose the best reply in response to B.

**A** Strange, I've never seen you here before.
Are those the people you're with?
Oh, just curious. It's always nice to see a new face.
**B** . . .
**A** Well perhaps we'll see each other again.
Oh, how fascinating. I'm an artist.
No, but I'd love to meet him.
**B** . . .

### CUE CARD B

You are by the swimming pool of an exclusive club. Choose the best reply to A.

**A** . . .
**B** Why do you ask?
Yes, I'm a member.
No, I'm here with friends.
**A** . . .
**B** No, they're inside. Do you know Sir Charles Stutton?
Well, I'm afraid I must go. My friends are waiting.
I don't have time to come too often. I'm a model.
**A** . . .
**B** Well, come on in and join us. I'm sure Sir Charles would be delighted to meet you. What's your name?
That's funny, my husband's an artist, too. Here he is now. Hello, John!
I doubt it.
Goodbye.

### REMARKS

If cue cards are used it is important that the conversation practised should stretch the students and be a little beyond their normal competence. The focus should also be on performance and students should be encouraged to make every attempt to get the intonation right. For this reason it might be useful to have readings of the dialogues available on tape. If possible, students should also be encouraged to record their conversations.

### VARIATION

A useful variant for more advanced students would be cards where students have the option of giving the same message in a number of different registers.

## 12 The phone game

**LEVEL** — **Elementary and above**

**TIME** — **10–15 minutes**

**AIM** — To give students controlled practice of telephone conversations.

**PREPARATION** — None.

**PROCEDURE**

**1** Write the following on the blackboard and ask your students to read it carefully:

Your girlfriend has left you an urgent message to ring Cambridge 312433. This is not a number she normally uses. Her name is Laura Higgins. Your name is John Roberts.

**2** Explain that John Roberts is going to try to get through to Laura Higgins. Take all the other roles yourself.

**3** During the activity you can nominate any one of the students to be John Roberts at any point. When a student is nominated he takes over the conversation. The activity might proceed as follows:

| | |
|---|---|
| **Teacher** | Cambridge 312433 (points to student A). |
| **A** | Please give me Ms Higgins. |
| **Teacher** | Who? (points to student B). |
| **B** | I wonder if I might speak to Ms Higgins? (Teacher indicates that there is a problem.) |
| **B** | (reformulates) I wonder if I could speak to Ms Higgins, please? |
| **Teacher** | Certainly, hold the line, please. |

**REMARKS**

As students gain confidence all kinds of problems can be built in including wrong numbers, more than one Ms Higgins, an answering machine, etc. Each time communication breaks down the teacher recycles all the exchanges up to the point of breakdown indicating inappropriate intonation, stress, vocabulary, word order, etc. by gesture and then the student tries again.

**Acknowledgement**
A version of this activity was presented by Celia Roberts at a seminar in the University of Lancaster.

# Exchanges

As the exchange is the basic unit of conversation there is a case for work which focuses on the exchange from the start. The following activities are controlled in that the choice of vocabulary and structures can be very restricted although the level of response required in fact draws on the students' full understanding of the language.

# 13 Who said it?

**LEVEL** **Intermediate and above**

**TIME** **15–20 minutes**

**AIM** To get students to interpret and attribute utterances.

**PREPARATION** Make photocopies of the following task sheet and the picture on page 36 for your class.

---

**TASK SHEET**

**Task 1**
Work in pairs. Look at the picture and decide who might be saying the following:

**a.** I told you not to wear a suit.
**b.** . . ., and the doctor says I'm pregnant.
**c.** Are you a friend of Jim's?
**d.** I thought Esmerelda looked terrible this evening. Didn't you?
**e.** How do you stand it? Have you complained?
**f.** And then he told me I was going to be promoted.
**g.** So I said 'Don't speak to me like that again . . .'

**Task 2**
Now decide what the other speaker might say as a response to the statements above. Compare your answers with the rest of the class.

---



**PROCEDURE**

1 Introduce the students to the idea of the task by asking them to guess who might be saying what in a visual, e.g. a photograph of someone hiring a car.

2 Divide the students into pairs and give out copies of the task sheet and picture. Students should need about ten minutes to complete the task.

3 Run a feedback session in which the pairs get a chance to exchange answers. Ask the students to practise the exchanges they have written. Concentrate on the rhythm and intonation.

**REMARKS** An optional extension of this activity would be to get students to try to develop a short dialogue (five or six lines) from one of the exchanges.

## 14 Split exchanges

**LEVEL** **Elementary and above**

**TIME** **10–15 minutes**

**AIM** To get students to focus on exchange structure.

**PREPARATION** Write one part of an exchange for each student in the class. Here are some examples. These would be enough for twenty students:

- What are you doing?
  Why do you ask?
- What's up?
  I've lost my contact lens.
- What was the film like?
  The photography was OK.
- I can't find my notes.
  Don't worry they'll turn up somewhere.

- The problem with teenagers today is they don't respect age.
  Oh, listen to you talk!
- Jack's leaving on the tenth.
  As far as I know.
- How's he feeling?
  No idea.
- I'm meeting someone on the flight from Delhi.
  Oh, I think it's just come in.
- Dinner's ready.
  Coming.
- Gosh it's hot in here today.
  I'm used to it.

**PROCEDURE**

**1** Give each student half an exchange on a sheet of paper. Give them a minute to memorize what is written on the sheet before the class circulates freely.

**2** Ask each person to say aloud only the words they have been given and then listen to what is said by the others to see if anyone might have the other part of their exchange. Tell the students they have to speak to everyone.

**3** After about five minutes ask those students who think they have found a partner to move to one side of the room. Those without partners call out their half of the exchange to the whole group and invariably two or three people will have parts of exchanges which go together.

**REMARKS**

This can be used at any level by varying the difficulty of the exchanges.

**Acknowledgement**
Alan Maley and Alan Duff, *Drama Techniques in Language Teaching* (CUP 1978, new edition 1982).

# Gambits

In the early stages of conversational development students can be taught to take the part of the person who responds to what somebody else has said, by producing an appropriate response or 'gambit'. This can be done by teaching them to use a variety of short responses that contribute to the maintenance of conversation. A list of what we might teach is as follows:

**1** Language to indicate the speaker's agreement with what has been said:

- *Yes, it is.*
- *Yes, that's right.*
- *Of course, it is.*
- *Quite, absolutely true.*
- *Yes, I do/Yes, he was/Yes, they were*, etc.

**2** Language which indicates polite disagreement:

- *Well, not really.*
- *Not quite, no.*
- *Perhaps not quite as bad/good/difficult as that.*
- *Em, I don't know.*

**Note:** The co-operative nature of conversation is such that disagreement tends to be expressed in a roundabout way.

**3** Language to indicate possible doubt:

- *I'm not quite sure.*
- *Really?*
- *Is that right?*
- *Is that so?*
- *Are you sure?*

**4** Language to provide positive and negative feedback:

- *Great!*
- *That's nice.*
- *Very nice indeed (good, clear, pretty)*, etc.
- *Really nice.*
- **Sounds lovely!*
- *Not very nice.*
- *Not at all nice/clear*, etc.
- *Very nasty indeed (disagreeable, bad, noisy), etc.*
- **Sounds awful.*

**5** Language to encourage confirmation and more information:

- *Is that right?*
- *Really?*
- **No kidding?*
- *You're not!*

* Denotes items which are particularly informal.
(See *Teaching the Spoken Language* by Brown and Yule, 1983.)

The following strategies also encourage more information:

- Using a pronoun and an auxiliary verb that refer to the subject and verb of the preceding statement or phrase, e.g.

  **A** I like your car.
  **B** *You do?*
  **C** Yes, I wouldn't mind buying it off you when you get a new one!

- Using a short question that repeats a key word or a phrase from the preceding statement:

  **A** Is it cold?
  **B** Not too bad, but it's raining.
  **A** *Raining?*
  **B** I'm afraid so. It's not too heavy though.

One way of getting students used to the function of short responses is to build them into drills. Students enjoy the challenge of getting the stress and intonation of the short response right, and adding a short response as the second or third part makes drills more complete and natural. Although such practice is semi-mechanical it is possible to add a measure of personal response. Students can also be encouraged to look out for these short responses in conversations they hear.

## 15 Anyone for tennis?

**LEVEL**

**Elementary to Lower intermediate**

**TIME**

**Drill for 5–10 minutes**

**AIM**

1 To enable students to practise *going to* to express the future.

2 To get students to provide an appropriate response to the answer to the previous question.

**TARGET EXCHANGE**

**A** What are you going to do this weekend?
**B** I'm going to play tennis.
**A** Oh, that's nice. I love tennis.

**PREPARATION**

Prepare the picture cues below.

?
weekend

?
Sunday

**PROCEDURE**

1 A's response to B is determined by A's attitude to the activity in question, and the first stage of this activity is to pre-teach the form and intonation of possible responses. These could include:

- *Oh, that's nice.*
- *Rather you than me, I hate tennis.*
- *Great, I love tennis.*
- *Lucky you, I'd love to play tennis,* etc.

2 Provide a language model to the class yourself and then prompt A's first question and B's reply by showing the cues to nominated students. The cards should have prompts for the questions written on one side, and picture prompts for the responses on the other.

3 Make the drill snappy and insist on appropriate intonation.

**REMARKS**

Encourage student A to express his or her own true feelings about the activity.

## 16 Is that right?

**LEVEL**

**Elementary and above**

**TIME**

**10–15 minutes**

**AIM**

To help students to recognize gambits.

**PREPARATION**

Find a short cassette or video recording of two or three people chatting naturally. Identify examples of short responses being used and put them in random order on a task sheet, blackboard or OHT, along the following lines. You can add distractors if you wish. The task sheet might look like this:

---

**TASK SHEET**

Read the following list of expressions. Listen to the tape. Tick (√) any of the expressions you hear. You may hear some expressions more than once:

| | | | |
|---|---|---|---|
| *Is that right?* | ______ | *That's great!* | ______ |
| *Really . . .?* | ______ | *Oh, dear.* | ______ |
| *How interesting!* | ______ | *What a shame!* | ______ |
| *Er . . . hum.* | ______ | *Oh, no!* | ______ |
| *Fine.* | ______ | *You're joking!* | ______ |
| *I see.* | ______ | | |

---

**PROCEDURE**

1 Give a task sheet to each student and ask them to tick off examples they hear on the tape.

2 When they have done this, choose two or three examples to focus on and see if the students can recall the utterances which precede or follow them on the tape.

## 17 Dialogue fill-in

**LEVEL**

**Intermediate and above**

**TIME**

**10–15 minutes**

**AIM**

To give students practice in producing more than minimal responses.

**PREPARATION**

Choose a dialogue in which one partner, (B), provides only a minimal response. For example:

**A** Hello, where are you from?
**B** From Singapore.
**A** Why did you come to London?
**B** To study.
**A** Oh, what are you studying?
**B** Accountancy.
**A** How long are you planning to stay?
**B** Two years.
**A** When did you arrive?, etc.

**PROCEDURE**

1 Read the dialogue to the students after setting the scene:
A is a British student who meets an attractive foreign student (B).

2 Ask your students why A is likely to lose interest in B? What is wrong with the conversation?

3 Once the students understand that B can help the conversation develop by adding a second part to the response, ask them to work in pairs to do the following:

– add questions or comments to B's answers;
– write in A's replies.

4 You should encourage your students to practise what they add verbally to see if it sounds natural. A selection of dialogues can be performed in a feedback session.

# Meaningful grammar practice

The ability to operate the structures and tenses of English is an important part of being able to produce language. As we are interested in developing conversation it is possible to concentrate our practice of grammar on forms which are commonly employed in conversation, and to make such practice meaningful by building in some element of personalization, individual investment, and information exchange into the task. The range of these activities is very wide, and the ideas which follow are meant to give an idea of what might be possible.

## 18 The best years of my life

LEVEL **Elementary and above**

TIME **10–15 minutes**

AIM To give students practice in the simple past forms.

PREPARATION None.

PROCEDURE

1 Ask the students to list five particularly personal significant dates on a piece of paper.

2 When they have done this divide them into pairs and ask them to exchange information using the following basic model which you should introduce before they start:

**A** I remember 1976. It was the year I had my accident. Do you remember it?

**B** Yes, it was the year I . . ./No, not really.

3 Go through a few examples with the whole class.

**Acknowledgement**
Mario Rinvolucri and Christine Frank, *Grammar in Action* (1983).

## 19 Experiences

LEVEL **Elementary and above**

TIME **15–20 minutes**

AIM To give students practice in the present perfect tense.

**PREPARATION**

None.

**PROCEDURE**

**Students studying in the UK or US**

1 Ask the students to list six new things they have done or seen since they have arrived.

2 Once they have done this, ask them to mingle to see if anyone else has seen or done the same things by asking questions such as:

- *I went to the Tower of London for the first time last week. Have you ever been?*
- *Have you seen any punks?*, etc.

3 Once the noise subsides, get feedback by asking if anyone has done or seen anything which nobody else has had experience of. If this is really the case, follow-up work could involve the students in telling the others about it.

**A mixed nationality class**

1 Ask the students to list five things/places/foods, etc. which are representative of their country. The class can then mingle and ask each other questions like:

- *Have you ever tried 'cous cous'?*
- *Have you ever been to Marrakesh?*
- *Have you ever heard of the Karyouine Mosque?*, etc.

2 Organize group or whole class feedback in the form of a report on the other students' state of knowledge about their country. Give them an opportunity to exchange information.

**REMARKS**

These activities are most suited to small multinational classes. Teachers working in monolingual classes could consider inviting native-speaker informants or allowing the students to interview them about their experiences.

## 20 Pet hates

**LEVEL**

**Elementary and above**

**TIME**

**10–15 minutes**

**AIM**

To give students practice in forms, such as *I love*, *I can't stand*, *I hate*, etc.

**PREPARATION**

Assemble on a cassette as rich and as varied a selection of music as possible.

**PROCEDURE**

1 Pre-teach or revise a number of utterances for expressing likes and dislikes. (These will vary according to the level of the class.)

2 After the revision, ask the students to react to each extract of music in turn, using the language forms above.

**REMARKS**

The advantage of using music is that it assaults the senses and demands a varied response.

**Acknowledgement**
The idea of using music was learnt from a presentation of the *Cambridge English Course* by Michael Swan and Catherine Walter, (CUP 1984).

## 21 The old days

**LEVEL**

**Intermediate and above**

**TIME**

**15–20 minutes**

**AIM**

To give students practice in using *used to*.

**PREPARATION**

Acquire old postcards, photographs, or prints of the town the students are living in, and combine them with recent photographs of the same site.

**PROCEDURE**

1 Revise *used to*.

2 Divide the class into small groups and use the visual material in order to discuss how things used to be. Ask each group to identify five to ten major changes.

3 Ask the groups to report back in turn.

**REMARKS**

A local industrial archaeology society is usually an excellent source of such material.

## 22 If only . . .

**LEVEL**

**Intermediate and above**

**TIME**

**10–15 minutes**

**AIM**

To give students practice in hypothetical *would*.

**PREPARATION**

Identify an area in which your students are able to list a number of complaints or recommendations quickly without much reflection.

(Students in the UK would probably respond to institutional food or landladies.)

**PROCEDURE**

1 Introduce the area for discussion and ask the students to list five complaints in the form of a statement using *would*, e.g.

- *I wish she would . . .*
- *If only they would . . .*

2 Go quickly round the class and ask the students for their ideas.

3 Write up new complaints as they occur and identify the most common ones.

**REMARKS**

Keep the tone light. Most students approach this in a spirit of fun, but sometimes serious problems can emerge, so follow them up if necessary.

## 23 Je ne regrette rien

**LEVEL**

**Intermediate and above**

**TIME**

**15–20 minutes**

**AIM**

To give students practice in hypothetical *would*.

**PREPARATION**

None.

**PROCEDURE**

1 Put the following list on the board or an OHT:

- *Your school.*
- *Your job or occupation.*
- *Your friends.*
- *Your habits, e.g. smoking, exercise, eating*, etc.
- *Your hobbies, e.g. playing the piano, stamp collecting*, etc.
- *Your skills, e.g. languages, carpentry*, etc.

2 Ask the students to write a personal entry for each heading, i.e. the name of their school, job, etc. They should then decide which of these they would or would not change if they were to live their lives again.

3 Once they have done this, encourage them to share their thoughts in small groups of three or four.

4 Ask the students to take it in turns to tell the others in the group what they would change if they had their life again. The others can ask questions and comment.

5 Wind up the activity by seeing if there are any areas that most of the class would want to change.

**REMARKS**

The title of the activity comes from an Edith Piaf song. There is an English version called 'No regrets'. It would make a lively and stimulating start to this activity.

## 24 Cheat

**LEVEL**

**Intermediate and above**

**TIME**

**10–15 minutes**

**AIM**

To give students practice in hypothetical *would*.

**PREPARATION**

Make photocopies of the following task sheet for your class.

---

**TASK SHEET**

**Cheating**
Work individually and read the following:

You are invigilating the English paper in a public exam. You have been told cheating is very common and during the exam you notice a blatant case of cheating. Candidates who are caught cheating in any subject fail all the others. The other examiners in the room are trying not to notice the problem.

Decide whether you would:

1 Report this to the senior examiner in the room and let him deal with it.
2 Ignore the problem like the others.
3 Approach the candidate and tell him to stop.
4 Confiscate the paper and report the student.
5 Read the rules on cheating to all the candidates again.

Choose someone else in the room and decide what he or she would do in the same situation. Ask the person to see if your decision was right.

---

**PROCEDURE**

1 Introduce the task and give out a task sheet to each student.

2 Ask them to read the task sheet individually and then work in pairs or small groups. Ask them to try to predict how the other members of the group would react or respond to the problem.

3 When they have done this give them a chance to check if they were right.

4 End the session by discussing the advantages and disadvantages of each option.

**REMARKS**

This type of activity works best with students who know each other well. It is an example of 'role reversal', and the same technique can be applied to any problem or questionnaire.

## 25 Could I ask you a few questions, please?

**LEVEL**

**Elementary and above**

**TIME**

**15–20 minutes**

**AIM**

To give students practice in question forms through the use of interview forms.

**PREPARATION**

Make photocopies of the model interview forms on pages 48/49 for the class. Alternatively, students can write their own.

**PROCEDURE**

1 Discuss and go through the questions the students might ask before letting them try the forms out on other members of the class.

2 Divide the students into small groups and give out the interview forms.

3 Make sure that the students are not in the position of having to answer questions they have just asked, by dividing the group or using more than one form.

4 Give students a chance to report back.

**REMARKS**

With mixed nationality groups it should be possible to systematically exploit cross-cultural issues, as in the examples here. It is also worth considering interviewing people outside the classroom setting.

**MODEL FORMS**

## Friends

Interview a student from a different country. Ask these questions about the person and the country he or she comes from.

| | | |
|---|---|---|
| Do you have friends of different nationalities or religions? | Yes ☐ | No ☐ |
| Are you typical? | Yes ☐ | No ☐ |
| Do you have friends of the opposite sex? | Yes ☐ | No ☐ |
| Are you typical? | Yes ☐ | No ☐ |
| Do friends go out in groups? | Yes ☐ | No ☐ |
| Are these groups mixed (male and female)? | Yes ☐ | No ☐ |
| Does a mixed couple usually go out alone or with other couples? | ________ | |
| Do you like going out in groups? | Yes ☐ | No ☐ |
| Do friends automatically become part of the family? | Yes ☐ | No ☐ |

Tick any of these which are *not* acceptable from friends:

- borrowing money; ☐
- visiting late at night; ☐
- arriving late for appointments; ☐
- not bringing a gift when they come for dinner. ☐

**Marriage**

Interview a student from a different country. Ask these questions about the person and the country he or she comes from.

|  |  | |
|---|---|---|
| Are you married? | Yes □ | No □ |
| When do people usually marry in your country? | under 20 | □ |
| | 20–25 | □ |
| | 25–30 | □ |
| | after 30 | □ |
| Do you have to pay to get a bride? | Yes □ | No □ |
| Do men and women choose their own spouses? | Yes □ | No □ |
| When you are married do you usually live with your family? | Yes □ | No □ |
| How many children do couples usually have? | ________ | |
| Where do people usually get married? | In a church | □ |
| | In a temple | □ |
| | In a registry office | □ |
| | Others(?) ________ | |
| Is it easy to get married in your country? | Yes □ | No □ |
| Is it easy to get divorced? | Yes □ | No □ |

# 3 Awareness activities

## Introduction

Students need to become aware of what native speakers *do* in conversation if they are themselves to achieve conversational competence in the target language. Such awareness can sometimes be acquired unconsciously as the result of prolonged exposure to the target language, but for many students the process could be facilitated and shortened by the use of activities which promote the following:

- the ability to 'sound' English by drawing attention to critical elements which can usefully be imitated, e.g. weak forms;
- development of the ability to interpret what is being said, and so facilitate interaction in the target language;
- a feeling for what is appropriate in conversation, and the effect it is having on the listener, in order to minimize problems in interaction;
- awareness of strategies used to further conversation so that these may be consciously adopted if desired;
- awareness of the target culture.

The activities which follow are based on the principle of discovery learning whereby observation and exploration form a base for imitation. It is, however, important for teachers using the activities to keep the overall aims in view and to avoid turning the exercises into a mini-course in applied linguistics. Provided the language of the task is simple and does not hinder the student from perceiving and becoming sensitive to how the language is being used, awareness activities can be used from the earliest stages of learning. With a little thought many of the activities which follow could be adapted for use with any class at any level. People who are in the early stages of language learning are often quite willing to make simple observations, to imitate and to experiment, while more advanced students will enjoy identifying, discussing, and imitating more subtle aspects of the language which they have previously been unable to capture. It is for these reasons that the regular inclusion of awareness activities from the start can prove both rewarding and productive.

When awareness activities are introduced for the first time it is a good idea for the teacher to give a simple explanation as to their purpose, and if necessary the initial activities could be done on a sample of the mother tongue so that the students become more familiar with the type of feature they are looking for. They may consequently be more sympathetic towards identifying similar features in the target language.

# Observation tasks

Observation tasks are used to encourage students to become sensitive to particular features of conversation. Observation should always be directed through the use of task sheets and these can be used to focus on:
- audio recordings of people talking;
- video recordings of people talking;
- conversations as they occur in real time.

The first group of observation tasks presented (pages 52 to 58) can be used with any data, but as observation in real time is extremely difficult it is better to avoid this unless the task is very clearly and simply defined. The simplest observation tasks require the observer to mark the presence (or absence) of a particular feature. The examples on pages 52 to 54 show how these tasks might be laid out. More sophisticated tasks may require students to identify further examples of expressions used to carry out a particular function (pages 54/5), or look at the interactional function of particular utterances (pages 55/6), and it is hoped that readers will use these examples to devise their own. A series of ideas for video-based tasks are also given on pages 58 to 62. These have the advantage of allowing students to focus on non-verbal behaviour such as gesture and body language, which may support certain linguistic features in conversation. However, video material of anything which resembles genuine, natural, everyday conversation is very rare, and it is important that the samples contain the features of conversation to be highlighted, unless the specific aim is to focus on their absence. There is therefore a need for careful preparation in using any of these tasks.

## 26 Encouraging noises

**LEVEL** **Elementary and above**

**TIME** **15–20 minutes**

**AIM** To make students sensitive to expressions which encourage the other speaker to continue.

**PREPARATION**

Select an audio or video tape that contains examples of this type of expression. Make photocopies of the following task sheet for the class. Add other items or distractors if necessary.

---

**TASK SHEET**

Listen to the extract of people talking. Make a tick (√) next to each of the expressions in the list whenever you hear one of the speakers using it.

| | | | |
|---|---|---|---|
| *Really?* | ________ | *Does he?* | ________ |
| *Is that right?* | ________ | *Is it?* | ________ |
| *That's nice.* | ________ | *Yes.* | ________ |
| *How interesting.* | ________ | *I see.* | ________ |
| *Uh huh.* | ________ | *Mmmm.* | ________ |

These expressions are often used to encourage the other speaker to say more. Is this true of the speakers you have been watching or listening to? Listen again and check your observations with a partner and with your teacher.

---



**PROCEDURE**

1 Introduce the task so that the students get some idea of what they are looking for.

2 Give out a copy of the task sheet to each student.

3 Play the tape two or three times before focusing on the specific expressions in context.

**REMARKS**

It is easy to find examples of such expressions in *Have You Heard . . .?* by Mary Underwood (OUP, 1979).

## 27 Keep talking

**LEVEL**

**Elementary and above**

**TIME**

**10–15 minutes**

**AIM**

To make students sensitive to the way in which fillers can contribute to an impression of fluency.

**PREPARATION**

Select a suitable audio or video tape and make photocopies of the following task sheet for the class.

**TASK SHEET**

Listen to the extract. Somebody is talking about something that has happened to them. Which of the following expressions does the speaker use in order to gain time to think of the next bit of the story, but also to keep talking, so that the listener knows that the speaker has not yet finished speaking:

| | | | |
|---|---|---|---|
| *Er, erm . . .* | __________ | *Anyway, . . .* | __________ |
| *Well, . . .* | __________ | *So you see, . . .* | __________ |
| *So, . . .* | __________ | *You know . . .* | __________ |
| *And then . . .* | __________ | *Know what I mean?* | __________ |

Which one does the speaker use most often? Compare your observations with a partner and then with your teacher.



**PROCEDURE**

1 Introduce the task and give out a copy of the task sheet to each student.

2 Play the tape two or three times, and if necessary, focus on the inappropriate use of certain fillers, for example, *You know*.

**REMARKS**

Any native speaker who is asked to tell a story or anecdote will produce a share of examples similar to those in the list. Another rich source is *What a Story!* by Mary Underwood (OUP, 1976).

## 28 Encouragement

**LEVEL**

**Intermediate and above**

**TIME**

**10–15 minutes**

**AIM**

To make students sensitive to expressions which encourage a speaker to say more.

**PREPARATION**

Select a suitable audio or video tape and make photocopies of the following task sheet for the class.

**TASK SHEET**

Questions that repeat a key word from what the other person has just said are used by native speakers to encourage the person to say more about the topic. For example:

**A** I usually go bowling.
**B** *Bowling?*

or

**A** What is the weather like in Portugal?
**B** Not so bad until it rains.
**A** *Rains?*
**B** Yes, I'm afraid so, but it doesn't last long.

Now do the following:

**a.** Listen to the extract and note down any examples of the same type of strategy. Discuss what you have written down with a partner.
**b.** Listen to the conversation again. What would have happened if the answer to the key word questions had been simply 'yes' or 'no' in each case?
**c.** Do you think that someone who simply answers 'yes' or 'no' sounds friendly, and interested in continuing the conversation?
**d.** Do *you* ask questions like this in conversation?
**e.** How do you respond to keyword questions?

Discuss your answers with a partner.



**PROCEDURE**

1 Introduce the task in order to make sure that the students know what they are looking for.

2 Play the tape twice and give the students a chance to discuss their answers in pairs or small groups before making any general points with the whole class.

## 29 Repetition

**LEVEL** **Upper intermediate to Advanced**

**TIME** **15–20 minutes**

**AIM** To help students become aware of the different uses to which repetition can be put in the spoken language.

**PREPARATION** Select suitable audio or video data and make photocopies of the following task sheet for the class.

**TASK SHEET**

Listen to the extract and find examples of speakers repeating something which has been said earlier in the conversation. When you have done this, consider the use of the repetition in each case. Discuss your ideas with a partner and use the following checklist to help you decide.

**1** The speaker repeats part of a question in order to be able to answer it.
Example from the extract: ................................................

**2** The speaker uses repetition in order to give himself or herself time to plan what he or she is about to say next.
Example from the extract: ................................................

**3** The speaker uses repetition to make sure that the listener is following.
Example from the extract: ................................................

**4** The speaker uses repetition to show agreement with what the other speaker has just said.
Example from the extract: ................................................

**5** The speaker uses repetition in order to encourage the other speaker to say more.
Example from the extract: ................................................

**6** Other (please specify).
Example from the extract: ................................................

**Note:** The extract you are listening to may not contain examples of all the uses listed above. It is up to you to decide whether to reduce the list or to add to it according to what you hear.



**PROCEDURE**

**1** Go through the task sheet with the students and introduce a few different examples so that they get the idea of the task.

**2** Give students a chance to listen to the data as many times as they need.

**3** Focus on some of the examples they identify.

**REMARKS**

Page 98 of *Teaching the Spoken Language* by Brown and Yule, (1983), contains a discussion of this.

# 30 As I was saying . . .

**LEVEL** **Upper intermediate to Advanced**

**TIME** **20–25 minutes**

**AIM** To focus the students' attention on types of interruption and how to deal with them.

**PREPARATION** Make enough photocopies of the following task sheets for each group of three students, i.e. each member of the group has a different task.

---

**TASK SHEET A** Spend a few minutes thinking of something interesting, exciting, funny, etc. which has happened to you or to someone you know. You can choose any subject you wish. When you are ready start telling the story to your partner.

---

**TASK SHEET B** Your partner is about to tell you a story. After about thirty seconds take any opportunity to interrupt him or her, e.g. because you don't understand, or you wish to make a comment, etc. The following expressions might prove useful:

- *Sorry, but . . .*
- *Excuse me, . . .*
- *Er, I'd just like to comment on that . . .*
- *Er, may I interrupt a moment . . .*

---

**TASK SHEET C** Your task is to observe what happens between the other two in your group. One is going to tell the other a story. The other, the listener, has been asked to interrupt as often as possible. As they speak try to note down:

**a.** How the interruptions are made.
**b.** What the storyteller's reaction is to the interruptions. Does he or she get angry? How does he or she deal with them? What does he or she say to try to get back to the story? Don't worry if you can't note down every example, just do as much as you can.

When the task is over discuss your observations with the other members of your group, and then be prepared to report what happened to the rest of the class.

---

**PROCEDURE**

**1** Divide the students into groups of three and give each student a task sheet. Make sure they do not look at each other's tasks.

**2** Explain that one student in each group will act as an observer, noting down what happens between the other two.

**3** When the task has been completed in the groups and they have held their own feedback sessions, chair a plenary session and ask for group reports. Introduce additional verbal strategies for dealing with interruptions, for example:

- *Where was I . . .?*
- *As I was saying . . .*
- *Yes, well anyway . . .*
- *To return to what I was saying . . .*
- *I'm sure that's true, but . . .*
- **May I continue?*
- **If you don't mind I'd like to continue . . .*
- **Is that all?*

The fact that the asterisked items are very strong and could be considered impolite should be noted.

**4** Centre the discussion on how to interrupt politely, as well as on circumstances when it is permissible to be less polite.

**5** Follow this up later with an interruption drill where you ask students to repeat bits of their story. Interrupt them politely or rudely. They have to counter the interruption appropriately. In particular, the intonation should be thoroughly practised here.

# Observation tasks based on video

The main advantage of using video is that, in addition to the language used, the students can also focus on the para-linguistic features which are often so crucial in getting meaning across. Some gestures and facial expressions are common to many language backgrounds, but others are not and it is these which the students can usefully learn to imitate and incorporate into their repertoire.

## 31 Gestures

**LEVEL**

**Intermediate and above**

**TIME**

**10 minutes**

**AIM**

To focus on the use of gestures as a reinforcement of what is being said.

**PREPARATION**

Select a video of a native speaker politician or public speaker. Make photocopies of the following task sheet for the class.

**TASK SHEET**

Look at the video of someone giving a talk. Are there any points where the speaker does the following?

| | | |
|---|---|---|
| **1** Raises or lowers his eyebrows. | Yes □ | No □ |
| **2** Nods or shakes his head. | Yes □ | No □ |
| **3** Uses his hands. | Yes □ | No □ |
| **4** Raises or lowers his shoulders. | Yes □ | No □ |
| **5** Stands up straighter. | Yes □ | No □ |
| **6** Visibly takes a deep breath. | Yes □ | No □ |

When he did the things you have noted, do you think he was:

- about to say something important;
- trying to emphasize what he was saying;
- trying to attract attention;
- trying to involve people in what he was saying;
- trying to do something else (please specify).



**PROCEDURE**

**1** The sort of video chosen should contain numerous examples of the speaker using the type of gestures mentioned in the task sheet to reinforce what he is saying.

**2** Play the tape through once or twice and see if the students can spot the gestures. Check the answers and run a discussion to highlight points such as the way in which many speakers mark important stress patterns with a movement of their body or hand.

**3** Explain to your students that with good speakers such movement is very finely co-ordinated with what they are saying at any point, and does not distract from the message (e.g. a speaker who is marking important points with a clear up and down movement of one hand is less distracting than someone who is randomly waving his or her hands about).

**REMARKS**

This exercise contributes to an overall sensitivity in students of how they should behave when speaking in public, and help them to restrict their hand movements in conversation if necessary. It also assists with the understanding and interpretation of what is being said, as attention to such clues should alert the students that what is to follow is important.

## 32 Follow me

**LEVEL** Elementary and above

**TIME** 15–20 minutes

**AIM** To get students to imitate the production of certain words and phrases, and the body language that accompanies them.

**PREPARATION** Find a short video recording in which one or more of the speakers are particularly expressive, (not more than two minutes).

**PROCEDURE**

1 Play the tape through once without stopping. Then play it through again, this time stopping after each utterance. Ask the students to imitate the way the utterance was said, as well as the accompanying body language.

2 Work slowly towards getting the students to reproduce a short section of the film and acting it out for the class, or in small groups.

3 Other students in the group can evaluate each performance against what was on the tape and award marks. The students who reproduce the language, intonation, and gestures most accurately win.

## 33 Sound off

**LEVEL** Elementary and above

**TIME** 10 minutes

**AIM** To help students use extra-linguistic clues to help them in understanding and interpreting what is being said.

**PREPARATION** Select a suitable video tape, (maximum of two minutes).

**PROCEDURE**

1 Play the tape through once with the sound turned off.

2 Ask the students to predict as much as they can about the verbal content of the extract from the visual images alone. This could involve guessing who the characters are, what they are talking about, what their attitudes are, etc.

3 You should encourage your students to give reasons for their answers on the basis of the setting, facial expressions, use of gesture, style of clothing, etc.

**4** Play the video through with the sound so that your students can check that their predictions were correct.

## 34 Sound only

**LEVEL** **Elementary and above**

**TIME** **Up to 20 minutes**

**AIM** To help students develop a feel for voice quality.

**PREPARATION** In many situations such as talking on the telephone, native speakers can be helped in their response to unknown speakers because they have a sense of the type of person they are talking to from clues in the speaker's voice. For example, the speaker may sound authoritative, educated, hesitant, uncooperative, etc. Therefore it is essential that you select a video which has a number of distinctive voices on it.

**PROCEDURE**

**1** Play the video extract with the picture covered or the monitor turned round.

**2** Ask the students to build up a mental picture of who is talking. The following prompts may help:

- Young/old?
- Male/female?
- Fat/thin?
- Well educated/poorly educated?
- Strong/weak?
- Confident/nervous?
- Co-operative/uncooperative?

(*Variations on a Theme* by Maley & Duff (1978), offers a series of ambiguous dialogues where students are asked to speculate on features like these.) More advanced students could listen for clues as to the speaker's character, e.g. the extent to which personal pronouns are used, the manner in which the speaker listens to and responds to questions, etc.

**3** This stage of the activity could be the basis of pair or small group discussion. After five to ten minutes ask the pairs or groups to report back to the rest of the class before playing the extract again with the picture, so that the students can check their hypotheses.

**4** A further discussion can then take place on the reasons for their observations and for these being right or wrong.

## 35 What's next?

**LEVEL** **Elementary and above**

**TIME** **Up to 15 minutes**

**AIM** To give students practice in following extended conversation, and in identifying vital cues which will help them to participate.

**PREPARATION** Select a video of two or three people holding some form of conversation. Authentic conversation is difficult to find on video, but extracts of drama productions will serve just as well and are perhaps easier for lower level students to handle.

**PROCEDURE**

1 Allocate each of the students the role of one of the speakers on the tape.

2 Start the tape and at appropriate points in the interaction stop the tape and ask questions such as:

- *Do you think he has finished what he has to say, or will he continue? How do you know?*
- *Who do you think will speak next? Why?*

3 When the next speaker has been established a student taking that role should try to predict what will be said.

4 The tape can then be played to check the students' predictions. The reasons for being right or wrong can then form the basis of a discussion.

**REMARKS** Predictive listening is an important part of being able to take part in a conversation. Many students turn off quite early on in conversations, especially where a number of people are involved. They are therefore unable to take a turn even when one is openly offered, and stand no chance at all of taking a turn at an appropriate pause, or in response to a provocative comment. This activity can help students sustain interest in a conversation for longer and begin to identify the cues which enable them to take an active part.

# Sensitivity to gesture and facial expression

It is also possible to focus on the use of gesture and facial expression without the use of video.

# 36 A smiling face?

LEVEL

**Intermediate and above**

TIME

**20–25 minutes**

AIM

To raise sensitivity in students to body language.

PREPARATION

None.

PROCEDURE

1 Divide the class into pairs. Each member of the pair should produce a sequence of three cartoon faces, e.g.

2 Ask each pair to swop their cartoons and try to supply 'speech bubbles' for the faces in front of them. The final version can be exchanged with other pairs and the fours can discuss to what extent they feel the words supplied are at variance with the facial expressions.

3 Ask the students to repeat the task, but this time the verbal message *must be* at variance with the facial expression.

4 This time the students should form groups of six or eight for discussion and should explore the possible non-verbal signals that they would use to convey the message intended in each cartoon. They should consider facial expression, body position, hand movements, etc.

5 Finally, ask each group to prepare a short sketch in which a message is conveyed non-verbally *or* where there is a contradiction between what is said in words and what the non-verbal signals say.

REMARKS

It is not uncommon for the face to contradict what is being said in words. For example, people sometimes convey to someone in the same room that they do not really mean what they are saying to someone else on the telephone. Similarly, the face can portray that there is little or no sincerity or enthusiasm behind what is being said.

# 37 The message is . . .

**LEVEL** Intermediate and above

**TIME** 15–20 minutes

**AIM** To enable students to recognize the function of gestures in English.

**PREPARATION** Make photocopies of the following illustrations for your class.

## PROCEDURE

1 Give each student a copy of the handout, and ask them to work in pairs to identify what each of the gestures illustrated might mean.

2 When they have exhausted the potential of this task, organize a feedback session in which the students get the opportunity to discover the various interpretations that have been allocated to the gestures throughout the class. (This will be especially interesting in a multilingual class.)

The following questions might help structure the session:

- *What do you think that each of these gestures means?*
- *Do you know of any others not mentioned here? What do they mean?*
- *Which ones would or could you use in England? Have you seen anyone using them?*

## REMARKS

Considerable variation on the interpretation of these gestures can be expected in a mixed nationality group, and this activity can generate a lot of discussion. However, it might be unwise to use it with immature students, as gestures which may be innocuous in one country may be an insult in another. For example, number 8, which is widely used to mean 'Wait' or 'Slowly' in the Arab World, can be insulting in Italy. The gestures which would be understood by speakers of English are:

Number 1, the 'thumbs up' sign means 'everything is all right' and is similar in meaning to number 3, which is more widely used in the USA. Number 4, the 'thumbs down' sign, would be understood as a rejection or refusal. Number 6 means 'good luck' and 'let's hope for the best', and there is a verbal equivalent which is, 'Keep your fingers crossed!'. Number 9, stroking the chin, indicates that the person is thinking carefully about a problem. Number 10 means, 'I do not know.' It often accompanies the expression, 'Search me!'. Finally, number 12 indicates that a person is regarded as crazy. It is normally only used when talking privately about a third person, but is more likely to be used as a joke.

The gestures which are not common to speakers of English are:

Numbers 2 and 5 are sometimes used to indicate that there is something strange or suspicious surrounding the topic of conversation. Number 7 suggests some sort of conspiratorial behaviour used between people who know each other well. (All of the above signs may be known in some parts of Britain, but they are not widely used.) Number 11 is the gesture for 'Hello!' as used by Italians. Some English speakers might confuse this with the wave that sometimes accompanies, 'Goodbye!'.

# Sensitivity to the sound system

How often do you notice, focus on, and/or correct the following in what your students say?

- Phonetic confusion, e.g. *p*in vs. *b*in.
- Problems with consonant clusters, e.g. str or nch.
- Interference from the written form, e.g. ha*l*f.
- Failure to use the weak form, e.g. /wɜː/ not /wə/.
- Incorrect word stress, e.g. *under*stand rather than under*stand*.
- Incorrect intonation.

If the answer to most of these questions is 'Not very often', it is possible that you are neglecting an important area of teaching and you might like to look at the general introductions to pronunciation teaching in the following: *Teaching Practice Handbook,* Gower and Walters (1983), *A Training Course for TEFL,* Hubbard *et al* (1983), *English Pronunciation Illustrated,* John Trim (1965), *Tree or Three?,* Ann Baker (1982), *Ship or Sheep?,* Ann Baker (1977).

If students are to 'sound English', not so much in the sense of a perfect accent, but in the sense of making themselves easily comprehensible, there is a need to work on their pronunciation, stress, rhythm, and intonation from the start. This is essential if students are to participate effectively in a conversation, and be readily understood, so that the listener is not having to re-interpret what is being said and compensate for inappropriate stress and intonation. For this reason we feel that work towards the building up of receptive and productive phonological competence should be incorporated into the normal teaching of structures, dialogues, texts, etc. from the earliest stages of learning, through the identification, highlighting and practice of significant examples of rhythm, stress, intonation and pronunciation (including contractions and weak forms), as and when it is appropriate.

Most students do listening comprehension work, so the following additional tasks can be used with little adjustment. They can be applied to unscripted or semi-scripted material:

- Write out the full forms of words such as *because, until*, etc. Explain that these words appear on the tape, but ask the students to tell you what they actually hear. This will encourage them to become sensitive to reduced forms.
- Focus on contracted verb forms such as *I'd, It's*, etc. and show how these would be expanded in the written form.
- Give more advanced students a short extract of an authentic recording and ask them to agree on a transcript of exactly what they hear.
- Give the class a transcript of the recording they have been working on. Ask them to listen to the recording and mark the transcript with '(+)' to indicate a pause, '(++)' to indicate a longer pause, and so on. The reasons for particularly long and significant pauses could then be discussed. These might include: time to think of what to say next (this is very common but note

how speakers do not lose their turn by letting their voice drop); short pauses at critical points to indicate meaning, e.g. *I'm afraid I don't know* (no pause) versus *I'm afraid* (++) *I don't know* (significant pause); and pausing to indicate a new piece of information, as well as the importance of what is to follow, e.g. *It's* (+) *five o'clock*.

# Specific tasks on stress and intonation

Lengthy but infrequent attention to stress and intonation is less effective than short tasks that are built into the overall teaching programme and used little and often as introductory 'warming up' activities, end of lesson relaxers, or simply as and when the need arises in response to errors. The following selection gives some idea of what might be possible.

## 38 I want a blue one!

**LEVEL** **Elementary to Intermediate**

**TIME** **10–15 minutes**

**AIM** To give students stress practice in the context of a drill.

**PREPARATION** Prepare twenty-seven little cards with a picture on each to cover all the possible permutations of the following colours, fabrics, and items of clothing. The items can be increased and/or varied if required:

| | | |
|---|---|---|
| red | woollen | dress |
| blue | cotton | shirt |
| black | nylon | sweater |

The cards should look like this:

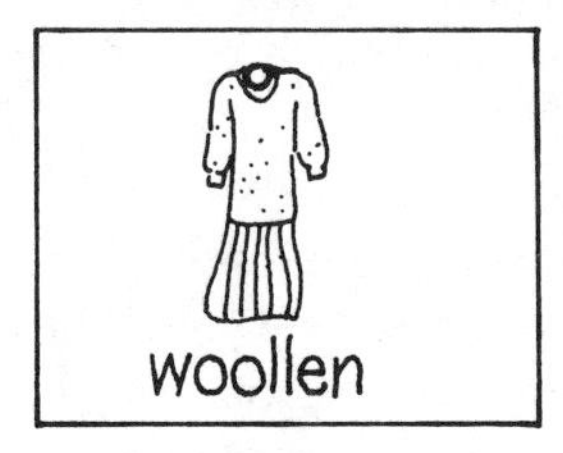


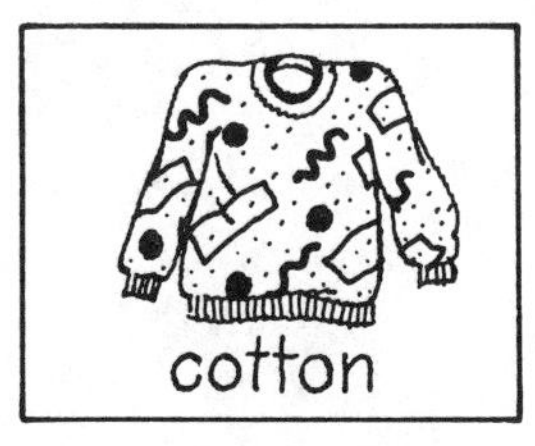


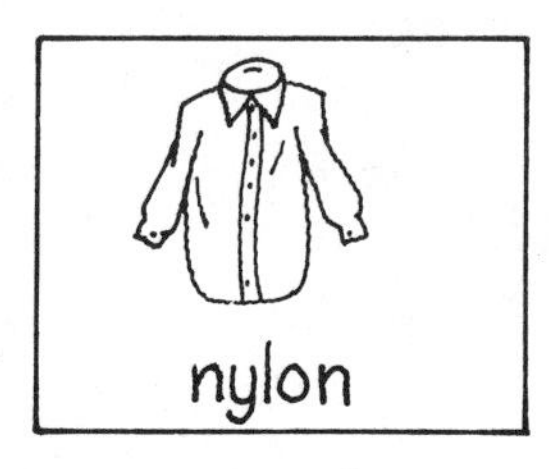


**PROCEDURE**

**1** Set up a shop situation. Show students the cards to indicate what they can buy, and write a substitution table on the board like this:

| | | |
|---|---|---|
| I'd like a | red woollen dress,<br>blue cotton sweater,<br>black nylon shirt, | please. |

2 Take the role of the shop assistant, and ask the students to take turns to ask for something in the shop. Whenever a student asks for something you should hand over a picture making an error in either the colour, the fabric, or the item of clothing. The student then has to correct the error using appropriate stress and intonation. The dialogue should go like this:

**Student** I'd like a red cotton dress, please.
**Teacher** Here you are.
**Student** No. I asked for a *red* cotton dress not a *blue* one.

or

**Student** I'd like a black woollen shirt, please.
**Teacher** Here you are.
**Student** No. I said a black woollen *shirt*, not a black woollen *skirt*.

3 When they have got the hang of the exercise divide the cards out among pairs of students so that they can practise on their own.

**REMARKS**

This activity could be used with other objects and adjectives.

## 39 I haven't got any ice!

**LEVEL**

**Intermediate and above**

**TIME**

**5–10 minutes**

**AIM**

To show students how shifting the stress in a prompted dialogue alters the meaning.

**PREPARATION**

Invent a model sentence and some prompts (see examples below). Rehearse acceptable responses privately before the lesson starts.

**EXAMPLE**

**Model** I haven't got any ice.
**Prompts** Ice and lemon, please!
Everyone's got some ice.
Please give me some ice!
Not even a little bit of ice?

**PROCEDURE**

1 Put a model sentence on the board.

2 Explain to the students that they should use this model sentence to reply to *all* the prompts given by you. The appropriacy of the reply is determined by where the students place the stress in the model sentence.

**Acknowledgement**
We are indebted to Beverly Sedley for the ideas used in the last two tasks.

# 40 Take that!

**LEVEL** **Intermediate and above**

**TIME** **15–20 minutes**

**AIM** To highlight and make students aware of sentence stress.

**PREPARATION** Prepare some short model dialogues illustrating strong emotion, and provide one small cushion for each pair or small group.

**PROCEDURE**

1 Divide your students into pairs or small groups. Give each pair or group a short dialogue which illustrates an emotion such as hate, anger, frustration, surprise, happiness, etc.

2 Ask the students to perform the dialogue as realistically as possible. When they get to the words carrying maximum stress they should throw the cushion at their partner(s), or in the air to express the emotion. As they do this the extra articulation that is required to speak *and* throw the cushion translates itself into the marked stress appropriate to the situation.

3 Swop the dialogues after a while. Here are some possible dialogues. The main stress is marked in each:

**Anger**
**A** Where were *you* last night?
**B** I was *out*.
**A** Oh! Who *with*?
**B** With *Joan*.
**A** Oh, I *hate* you.

**Frustration**
**A** Please stop that *noise*.
**B** I won't be *long*.
**A** It's *annoying* me.
**B** Just hang *on*.
**A** I said *stop* it!

**Happiness**
**A** I've got the *job*!
**B** Oh, that's *wonderful*.

**REMARKS** This activity is particularly useful with students whose mother tongue is a syllable-stressed language and who consequently tend to speak English monotonously and with little voice movement. It can also help very shy and reserved students to overcome some of their inhibitions about speaking in a foreign language. Extroverted classes too will benefit from and enjoy being given the opportunity to express strong emotions in a foreign language, and will quickly discover how flat their responses tend to be normally. Nevertheless, it is wise to warm students up with other drama techniques, such as those in *Drama Techniques in Language Learning* by Maley and Duff (1978), before using this one.

**Acknowledgement**
We first heard of this activity from Elayne Phillips.

## 41 This is a question?

LEVEL

**Upper intermediate and above**

TIME

**20–25 minutes**

AIM

To make students sensitive to how intonation can alter meaning.

PREPARATION

Prepare a set of simple utterances, such as:
- *Peter bought the house yesterday.*
- *The school is only six miles from the centre*, etc.

PROCEDURE

**1** Divide the class into small groups. Give each group three or four simple utterances, and ask them to work out as many different ways of saying them as possible. The meaning should be slightly different in each case.

**2** Ask one member of each group to speak the different versions of the sentence that the group has agreed upon.

**3** After a discussion with the class, write up the different meanings of the versions given, on the board. Make sure that all the versions are in fact acceptable, and encourage the different groups to challenge one another.

**4** By the end of the session the use of intonation to distinguish between statements, questions, commands, and exclamations, etc. should be clearly established.

## 42 Same words – different message

LEVEL

Stage 1 can be used with intermediate students. The other stages are more appropriate to advanced groups.

TIME

**15–20 minutes** for each stage.

AIM

To familiarize the students with the ways in which the meaning of an utterance can be altered by changing the intonation.

PREPARATION

Prepare a dialogue along the lines of the following example:

**A** Where were you last night?
**B** Why?
**A** Well, I rang at ten o'clock and you weren't in.
**B** No. I went to the cinema.
**A** Oh really? Who with?
**B** Just an old friend from university.
**A** Oh.

**PROCEDURE**

**Stage 1**

**1** Read out or record two versions of the dialogue you have prepared, or the one given above.

**2** In one recording or reading the dialogue is between two casual friends. In the other it is between a jealous boyfriend and his girlfriend. Ask your students to try to determine which is which by listening to the differences in intonation, stress, etc.

**3** Now ask the students, in turn, to identify the differences in stress and intonation by imitating the utterances which differ greatly between the two dialogues.

**4** When they do this ask the other members of the group to offer suggestions for improving the intonation and stress, where appropriate.

**Stage 2**

**1** Divide your students into small groups. Ask each group to decide on a reading for a given dialogue. The dialogue should not be punctuated and ideally should consist of very short utterances, for example:

**A** Come in
**B** Got it
**A** But yes
**B** From him
**A** Yes he had it

**2** Ask each group to prepare and then perform its version and if possible record it.

**3** Play the different versions to the class so that they can decide on an interpretation for each one, i.e. relationship of speakers, mood, attitude, aims, and intentions, etc. Any differences between the interpretation and what the group intended should be brought up for discussion.

**Stage 3**

**1** Still in their groups, ask the students to produce their own dialogues along the lines of the one in stage 2. Each dialogue should not be punctuated and the utterances should be fairly short.

**2** Ask each group to swop their dialogue with another group. Each group should decide on an interpretation of the dialogue it has received and work out a performance of it for the rest of the class. Again any difficulties the class has in interpreting the dialogue, or any differences between the writers' intentions and the interpretation given should be discussed.

**REMARKS**

It would not be appropriate to use all three stages of this activity in one session. Moreover, stages 2 and 3 can be omitted altogether if they are considered too difficult for the group. It is important that the students taking part in this activity already have some awareness of the significance of intonation in English, even if they still find difficulty in identifying or imitating particular features. The activity will be more successful if a tape recorder is available for recording the different versions of the dialogues so that repeated listening is possible. This encourages attention to detail and correctness, and provides material which can be worked on at the feedback stage.

## Cross-cultural awareness

The extent to which we should expect students to 'become English' by developing an English accent, adopting English values, absorbing English culture, etc. during the process of their language learning is a political issue, and the extent to which cross-cultural training should form a part of the language learning programme will probably be dependent on the students' objectives and the teacher's knowledge and motivation. For example, a student who is learning the language in order to settle in an English-speaking country is likely to be more interested in learning the social rules of communicating in English than the student who is learning English for a specific job purpose where he or she is unlikely to want to do more than read manuals. Similarly, a native-speaker teacher is probably in a better position to help the first student, although this is not always the case. However, if we accept the fact that language is embedded in culture, then some element of cross-cultural training is inevitable and the inclusion of some cross-cultural work in the teaching of conversation would seem to offer the following advantages:

- Cross-cultural issues can be generative of discussion in their own right.
- Knowledge of why people in the culture of the target language behave in certain ways should make native speakers more approachable and easier to interpret.
- A sensitivity to the ways social norms operate in other languages should make the learning of certain areas of language such as politeness formulae, easier.
- If students become aware of issues such as social taboos, they are less likely to cause offence by breaking them. By the same token they may well find themselves generating more input, because they begin to fall into the category of foreigner that native speakers find easy to talk to.

The content of a cross-cultural programme will vary considerably according to the circumstances, and the exercises which follow serve to illustrate some of the techniques which can be adapted for use with different content.

# 43 True or false?

**LEVEL**

**Upper intermediate to Advanced**. (However, if the statements are simple enough this activity could be used with any level.)

**TIME**

**25–30 minutes**

**AIM**

To familiarize students with ways in which native speakers try to be polite in social encounters.

**PREPARATION**

Make photocopies of the following task sheet for your class, or if you prefer, make it into an OHT.

---

**TASK SHEET**

**True or false?**

**1** It is considered impolite if you do not say 'please' when you bump into somebody accidentally in a corridor, or a crowded place.

**2** In England people do not automatically shake hands when they meet for the first time.

**3** When you answer the telephone in England you should always start by giving your name.

**4** When you go into a shop in England you should always address the shopkeeper as 'sir' or 'madam'.

**5** If you want to attract the attention of someone you do not know you should use 'sir' with a rising intonation.

**6** When you want to attract a waiter in a restaurant in England you should snap your fingers and say 'waiter' in a loud voice.

**7** When you enter a railway compartment or a room which is full of strangers in England, you should greet each of the people present. You will be considered impolite if you do not.

**8** When you greet someone in England it shows your concern if you ask after their health.

**9** Requests should usually be followed by 'please', except in public situations such as a pub or café where it is sufficient to state your order clearly, e.g. 'A beer'.

**10** When you are on the phone it is normal to signal that you are about to end a conversation by using expressions such as 'Look, I've got to go', or 'I'll let you get back to what you're doing'.

**11** In England it is polite to ask a person's age or salary as a way of getting to know them.

---

**PROCEDURE**

1 Divide your students into pairs. Give a task sheet to each pair and ask them to decide whether they think the statements are true or false. If they think a statement is false they should try to work out what should be said or done in the particular situation.

2 After the students have had a chance to discuss all the statements in pairs, organize and chair a feedback session. Some of the points which may emerge include:

- Statements 2 and 10 are basically true. In 2 discussion may centre around why the English appear standoffish when meeting someone for the first time. They tend to observe a very reserved greetings procedure in comparison with many other cultures, which may emphasize kissing, prolonged handshakes, etc. Discussion of 10 should bring out the fact that many non-native speakers of English often seem very impolite because of their tendency to bring conversations to a sudden halt. The need for 'pre-closings' should emerge.
- Statements 1 and 5 serve to draw attention to the correct use of 'Excuse me', 'I'm sorry', and 'That's all right'. Students at this level will probably be aware of the expressions but may not use appropriate intonation or choose the right expression for the right situation. (See *Practical English Usage* by Michael Swan, (1980).)
- Statement 3 provides an opportunity to revise telephone answering procedures. In a private home the person answering the phone would probably simply say 'Hello' or give the number.
- Statement 4, and to some extent 5, emphasize the problem caused by the fact that English has no neutral or formal term of address. In 4 an ordinary greeting such as 'Good morning', would be all that was necessary; 'sir' or 'madam' would be reserved for a client. For attracting an unknown person's attention a loud but polite 'Excuse me' is probably the most likely. Generally speaking, attracting a waiter (statement 6) is best done discreetly with the use of a hand signal and possibly a quiet and polite 'Waiter' if he is not too far away. Finger snapping and shouting are considered rude, and would normally only be used in the event of very bad service and total inattention from an underworked waiter.
- While people sometimes address a general greeting (statement 7) to a group of strangers it would be considered intrusive to greet people individually. Eye contact and a smile to acknowledge the majority of people in the group is sufficient. When entering a railway compartment it is common practice to ask 'Is this seat taken?' even when it obviously is not. This serves as a way of acknowledging the presence of the other people in the compartment (or similar area).

- Questions which ask specifically about health are also considered intrusive (statement 8) except with close friends and relatives, and generally the formulaic 'How are you?' is sufficient. A detailed and specific response to this question is not normally required or expected.
- Statement 9 draws attention to the fact that requests should always be mitigated by the use of politeness formulae such as 'please', 'would you mind?', etc. and that when these are absent the native speaker to whom the request is addressed will probably be offended and tend to respond in an uncooperative manner.
- Finally, statement 11 would be considered extremely rude, and a more general approach to getting to know someone should be used such as 'Where do you work?' and 'How long have you worked there?'.

**REMARKS**

1 Not everyone will agree as to which habits are 'typical'.

2 The same activity can be used with lower level students using simpler statements.

## 44 Similarities and differences

**LEVEL**

**Upper intermediate to Advanced** (depending on the wording of the task).

**TIME**

**20–25 minutes**

**AIM**

To make students sensitive to social behaviour in the target language.

**PREPARATION**

Make photocopies of the following task sheet for the class, or make it into an OHT.

## TASK SHEET

Think about situations in your country when you want to do each of the following. Consider the questions in each section and make notes in your group on what people normally do. Add any other information which you think might be of interest to other students who do not know your culture very well.

What do you usually do when you:

**1 Greet someone?**

**a.** What do people typically say? Try to translate it into English.
**b.** Do people shake hands, kiss, etc?
**c.** Is there an order to what people do? Do they shake hands before, during, or after the greeting? Which cheek do they kiss first?

**2 Compliment someone?**

**a.** In your country would you expect someone to compliment you:
- when you buy a new car;
- when you've just been to the hairdressers;
- when you are wearing something new or special;
- when you do something well;
- when they visit your home for the first time;
- when you've just made them a meal.

**b.** What do people say in each of the above situations?
**c.** Are there any gestures that you use when you compliment someone?
**d.** Would you compliment a stranger? Who? When? Where?

**3 Apologize to someone?**

**a.** In which of these situations would people expect you to apologize in your country?
- when you arrive after the appointed time of a meeting, dinner, etc;
- when you telephone someone after 10.00 p.m.;
- when you have forgotten something you were expected to bring;
- when you walk into someone accidentally;
- when you offer someone a drink or a meal;
- when you break something which does not belong to you.

**b.** What would you actually say in each case?

**4 Criticize someone?**

**a.** When is it appropriate to criticize someone in your country?
**b.** What would you criticize people for? For example, their dress, their work, their attitudes, etc.
**c.** Would you be direct in your criticism or very indirect?

**PROCEDURE**

1 Ask the students to work individually or in small groups. In a multinational group students should work in their national groups.

2 When the task has been completed each group should report its findings to the rest of the class.

3 In the discussion which follows draw out, and focus on, the major differences between cultures and elicit what is known about conventions in English for each of the situations. If you are a non-native speaker, it might be useful to invite a native speaker informant to the lesson to add authenticity and interest to the lesson.

**REMARKS**

Each one of the tasks above can take some time to complete if they are to be done properly. It would therefore be a mistake to ask students to cover more than one area per lesson.

## 45 Culture shock!

**LEVEL**

**Intermediate and above**

**TIME**

**25–30 minutes**

**AIM**

For students to discuss the problems people encounter when they have to live in a new country for a period of time.

**PREPARATION**

Make photocopies of the task sheet over the page for your class.

**PROCEDURE**

1 Introduce the topic and give out a task sheet to each student.

2 Divide the students into small groups after they have had the chance to complete the task sheet individually.

3 Chair a feedback session to see what generalizations emerge. Remain as neutral as possible throughout.

4 If students have not had experience of living in a foreign country, you can ask them to imagine how strangers might feel. Small groups of students could also interview foreign informants.

**REMARKS**

If students going to an English-speaking country to study English realize that settling-in problems occur anywhere, and are encouraged to put them in perspective, learning should be promoted.

**TASK SHEET**

Here are some difficulties people encounter when living in a new country. Please indicate with a tick (√) how important each one has been or would be for you.

| | Of very great importance | Of great importance | Of some importance | Of no importance |
|---|---|---|---|---|
| **1** Differences in the weather | | | | |
| **2** Being away from the family | | | | |
| **3** Differences in the food | | | | |
| **4** Differences in the way people make friends | | | | |
| **5** Transportation problems | | | | |
| **6** Getting used to new ways of learning | | | | |
| **7** Adjusting to new ways of doing things, e.g. shopping | | | | |
| **8** Difficulties in communicating one's ideas | | | | |
| **9** Different living conditions | | | | |
| **10** Different social customs | | | | |
| **11** Getting newspapers and magazines from home | | | | |
| **12** Meeting people from the same country | | | | |
| **13** Knowing what to do in everyday situations | | | | |
| **14** Other (please specify) ______ | | | | |

# 4 Fluency activities

## Introduction

In the introduction to this book it was argued that an authentic response needs to be generated if students are to be trained in becoming good conversationalists in a foreign language. It can be argued too, that the conversational needs of the average foreign student fall within a limited range of purposes, the most important of which are:

- the maintenance and development of social relationships;
- information exchange;
- co-operative problem-solving in English;
- expressing ideas and opinions.

The aim of this chapter is to present tasks which help promote such behaviour.

If students are to achieve conversational competence the practice tasks they are given *must*:

- provide the experience of using English in real time, (i.e. people do not wait for the right or the appropriate answer in real life, as is often the case in the classroom).
- offer them the chance to express their own attitudes, emotions and ideas, etc. (i.e. so that they are motivated to use the language).
- provide the opportunity of using the language for a specific purpose, (i.e. there is a genuine need to achieve something through using the language and therefore mistakes matter).

It is also important that the tasks are culturally appropriate and perceived as relevant by the students. Therefore, although the tasks which follow can be used with little modification or preparation, teachers are encouraged to view this collection as a store from which they can select task types to be modified to suit the specific needs of their own students.

## Introducing fluency activities

The successful introduction of fluency activities to a class which has not encountered them before, usually requires an element of learner training. This is because a great many foreign students are used to an approach to language teaching (and to education in general), where it is assumed that:

**1** It is the teacher who initiates language exchanges.

**2** The student's task is to respond to the teacher.

**3** The teacher judges whether or not the student's performance is acceptable and provides immediate feedback.

Fluency activities, however, place the burden on the student and emphasize that:

**1** It is the student who initiates and determines what he or she wants to say (albeit within a framework or set of guidelines).

**2** Feedback can be delayed because the teacher is expected to keep a low profile throughout the activity in order to allow the student to become involved in using the language beyond the level of individual isolated sentences.

Consequently it is no surprise that student insecurity, caused by suddenly being expected to produce more than the isolated, and often predictable, sentence, provokes apparent disinterest, lack of participation and, in some cases, even downright hostility. Even where students take part in and enjoy the activities they may accuse the teacher of not teaching, because what they have been doing is unconventional. This sets up an unnecessary tension between teacher and student. There is insufficient space here for a comprehensive discussion of learner training, but it is hoped that the following guidelines will allow teachers to formulate their own approach.

Basically, learner training needs to cover the 'how' and the 'why' of what the students are being asked to do. The 'why' refers to the rationale behind the activities, and this may be particularly important where adolescent and adult students are concerned. Fortunately, *learning by doing* is intuitively satisfying, so students can often be painlessly weaned away from more traditional approaches and practices by the teacher's simply pointing out the ways in which these activities are helping to promote the objective of oral competence by forcing them to *use* the English they have in their heads. This needs to be coupled, however, with a balance between over-correction of errors and no correction of errors at all, so that the students may develop their confidence in using the language without feeling that the teacher is no longer interested whether mistakes are made or not. When doubts about fluency exercises arise, a constant appeal to the students' common-sense often works better than self-justification or an 'issue-raising' discussion about the language learning process, as many students feel inadequate in such discussions, and therefore resentful, because they do not have equivalent specialist knowledge and linguistic expertise.

The 'how' refers to the fact that students may not know exactly what is expected of them during the activity, or how they might make best use of what they are doing. It is therefore vital that, in the early stages of introducing fluency activities, the students perceive elements in common with what they have been used to, for example, the control procedures for setting up the activity, checking that instructions have been understood, knowing when to start, etc. In this way the range of activities which the students are able to take part in can gradually be extended. But this process may take hours or even weeks depending on the students' previous experience and expectations. It is therefore important for the teacher to remain patient, remembering that methods of learning are habits, and that habits can be difficult to change.

Littlewood in *Communicative Language Teaching* (1981), suggests that there is a continuum of classroom activities to promote communicative competence.

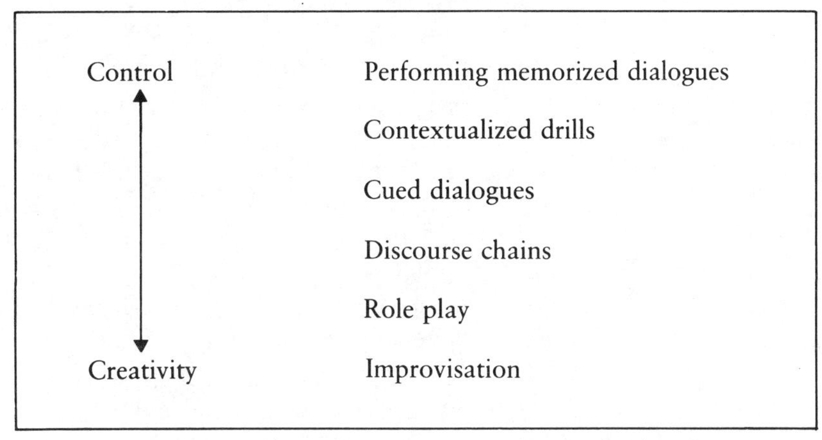


**Figure 2** *Continuum of activities to promote communicative competence*

Chapter 2 exemplified some of the more controlled activities and these can be used to help familiarize students with working together in pairs and groups in a relatively secure environment, before they are exposed to the added burden of creating their own contributions to the activity. Students will vary in terms of their previous learning experiences, and some may require very little preparation before they can work independently and creatively. This may be particularly true of children who are learning a foreign language for the first time as they are very willing to take risks and improvise. Adults may take considerably longer to adjust.

## Using fluency activities with monolingual classes

In monolingual classes teachers may find that students will readily revert to using the mother tongue in the execution of fluency activities. Indeed they may refuse to use the target language at all if not under scrutiny by the teacher. Some of the reasons for this problem include:

- social unease at using a foreign language with their peers;
- perceiving the task as being difficult to complete in any language;

- becoming so involved in the task that there is a genuine need to use the quickest and easiest way of communicating about the solution, i.e. the mother tongue. This is known as affective involvement.

Nevertheless, fluency activities can be used successfully with monolingual classes and the following advice may help with their introduction.

**1** Give the students a *reason* for using English in the completion of a task. In part this means explaining the rationale of the exercise, and for the rest it is a case of making the task *purposeful*. This means that the students must perceive a reason for doing the task other then the teacher simply telling them to do it.

**2** Start by asking the students to work in English for very short periods at a time and for relatively easy tasks. It is important not to be too ambitious in the early stages. When students accept this form of activity the length and difficulty of the tasks may gradually be increased. The activity should never appear threatening or stressful to the students.

**3** Praise students who make the effort to use English and who do not easily revert to the mother tongue.

**4** Make it clear to students that for this particular type of exercise errors are not so important. Keeping going in English is important, and although they should try to be accurate when they can, the teacher will not be listening for every little mistake. Prove this by praising those who string several sentences together, even when there are a number of errors.

**5** Prove to students that they can use English, by asking them to discuss and talk about their experiences of doing the task. This might include identification of what they found easy and difficult to express in English.

**6** Ask students to discuss and reflect upon what they used the mother tongue for during the exercise. Prove that with a little more thought and effort they could have found a way of saying it in English.

An unqualified 'English only' rule could be counterproductive if the students end up feeling frustrated if they cannot help each other to clarify points and get over minor difficulties in the instructions, etc. In fact, in the early stages of fluency activities, it is often reassuring for students if the task has an element of lexical or textual input, as well as an opportunity for feedback in the mother tongue, so that they perceive a link with more familiar, traditional activities. Maintaining this link through an element of formality in the treatment of a text providing input, or in the presentation of a group report after each task, will prevent the students from feeling that the activity has been a waste of time. As the students become more confident in their use of English, and as participating in freer and more creative activities becomes more of a habit, the formal element can be reduced and even discarded.

# Sharing

This section presents some activities which are designed to get students to share their private store of experience and their personal opinions with one another. A great deal of motivating language practice can be generated by asking students to talk about themselves, providing they have a framework in which to do so. The framework, especially in the early stages, should limit the exchanges to quite simple factual information which is not threatening or embarrassing to reveal, but which is nevertheless of interest to others. Such exchanges constitute a natural information gap activity in which all students are able to participate, without recourse to specialized knowledge, or the ability to think themselves into an imagined situation, or role. It is often the perceived lack of knowledge, and the blank mind when asked to invent that causes students to clam up and say nothing in the foreign language classroom. By contrast, being asked to talk about simple, practical, everyday experiences such as those which appear in the following exercises, can free the tongue of the most inhibited and reluctant student.

## 46 I hated Maths – did you?

LEVEL **Elementary and above**

TIME **25–30 minutes**

AIM To introduce students to fluency activities.

PREPARATION Prepare a task sheet along the following lines, and make photocopies for your class.

**TASK SHEET**

Look at this list of subjects we study in school:

| | | |
|---|---|---|
| English | Mathematics | Art |
| Geography | Physics | Physical Education |
| Chemistry | Biology | Literature |
| History | | |

Work individually for five minutes. Choose one of the subjects you particularly liked, and list three reasons for liking this subject. Choose one of the subjects you particularly disliked, and list three reasons for disliking this subject.

Now go round the class and find out if anyone liked or disliked the same subjects as you. Find out the reasons people gave for liking or disliking a subject and make a list under the headings below:

| **Reasons for liking a subject** | **Reasons for disliking a subject** |
|---|---|
| | |



**PROCEDURE**

1 Warm your students up for the task by getting them to list the subjects they did in school. This will check that they know the names of the subjects in English.

2 Give each student a task sheet and explain they have a maximum of fifteen minutes to get round the class. When they have finished, run a feedback session for the whole class and ask questions such as:

- Who liked/disliked the same subjects?
- What were the most common reasons for liking/disliking particular subjects?

Get the students to expand and comment on the reasons given.

**REMARKS**

The list of subjects needs to be made sensitive to the educational system the students have come from. Change the verbs to the present tense if the activity is to be used with adolescents.

## 47 Habits

**LEVEL** **Intermediate and above**

**TIME** **30–35 minutes**

**AIM** To get students to share opinions.

**PREPARATION**

Prepare a task sheet along the following lines, and make photocopies for your class.

**TASK SHEET**

**Task 1**
Some of our habits can be very annoying to other people. (For example, there was a case where a woman got a divorce because her husband ate spaghetti in bed!) Quite often it is small things that annoy people most.

Work in a group of four and look at this list of habits. Do any of them annoy you? Which ones? Why? Tell the group about it.

People who:
- bite their nails;
- lose their keys all the time;
- leave things lying around a room;
- smoke during a meal;
- play nervously with small objects, such as paperclips or elastic bands;
- play music very loud;
- use a personal stereo in crowded public places;
- never keep appointments on time;
- talk all the time;
- crack their finger joints;
- tap their fingers or their feet while you are talking to them.

Tell the others in your group about any other habits that you particularly dislike. Was there any agreement in your group? Choose one person in your group to tell the rest of the class about the habits that your group dislike most.

**Task 2**
Do you think *you* have any bad habits? Make a list and tell the group about them. Have they noticed them before? Tell each other about habits you want to change or have tried to change.

**Task 3**
Usually we accept habits even when they drive us mad. But sometimes, especially if we know the person very well, we may decide to talk to them to try and stop them from doing the thing that annoys us. Have you ever tried to stop someone from doing something that annoys you? Tell the group about it. What did you do? Was it successful? Do you think it is a good thing to try to change other people's habits?

**PROCEDURE**

1 Orientate your students to the task by asking for examples of habits.

2 Divide the students into small groups and give out the task sheet.

3 Allow the groups up to twenty minutes to run through the tasks.

4 End the session by getting the groups to tell each other about their discussion.

## 48 Family life

**LEVEL**

**Intermediate and above**

**TIME**

**25–30 minutes**

**AIM**

To get students to share opinions.

**PREPARATION**

Prepare a task sheet along the following lines, and make photocopies for your class.

---

**TASK SHEET**

Work in groups of three or four. Decide which of the following statements you agree with and which statements you disagree with. Discuss these with the other members of your group. Try to modify any statements you disagree with so that they represent the opinions of your group. Be ready to report your discussion to the teacher.

1 Children should only leave home after they are married.

2 Old people should be encouraged to stay in old people's homes rather than with the family.

3 People should not have more then two children.

4 Children should always obey their parents.

5 You should always ask your parents for permission to marry.

6 Children should pay their parents rent when they get a job.

7 You should always be ready to help a member of the family.

8 The members of a family should live in the same area so that it is easy for them to visit each other.

9 Family life is less important in the modern world than it was in the past.

---

**PROCEDURE**

1 Give out a task sheet to each student.

2 Divide the students into small groups and ask them to discuss the task sheet.

3 After about twenty minutes run a feedback session in which students report on the extent to which there was agreement or disagreement in the groups, and how they modified the statements.

**REMARKS**

Teachers should not use an activity like this with a group that is either intolerant or recently formed, because the opinions expressed may be intensely personal. The technique of statement modification can be used with any social issue likely to be of interest to students and the propositions can be adapted to take account of specific issues that may affect some groups more than others, e.g. arranged marriages.

## 49 Emotions

**LEVEL**

**Intermediate to Upper intermediate**

**TIME**

**30–35 minutes**

**AIM**

To get students to tell each other about their emotions.

**PREPARATION**

Prepare a task sheet along the following lines, and make photocopies for your class. If possible, have some dictionaries available.

---

**TASK SHEET**

How many of the following words do you know the meaning of?

| | | |
|---|---|---|
| joy | grief | terror |
| fear | sadness | worry |
| excitement | shame | relief |
| hate | triumph | love |
| affection | passion | pity |

They are all used to describe emotions. Work out what they mean with the help of a partner. Use a dictionary to help you if necessary.

Now think of as many events from the first eight years of your life as you can. Divide these into pleasant memories, unpleasant memories, or neutral ones. Can you remember the emotions you felt at the time? Use some of the words from the above list to describe the experiences. Tell your partner about a pleasant event and an unpleasant event from your childhood.

---

**PROCEDURE**

1 Introduce the discussion by getting the students to identify the emotions felt by people in news photographs, e.g. the joy of someone winning at Wimbledon, the sorrow of an earthquake victim, etc.

2 Give out the task sheet and monitor the vocabulary learning task. If possible, make dictionaries available.

3 Give the students up to fifteen minutes to complete the rest of the task.

4 End the activity by giving the pairs a chance to share their discussion in groups of four to six students.

## 50 A coma kit

**LEVEL** **Intermediate and above**

**TIME** **Up to 20 minutes**

**AIM** To get students talking about likes and dislikes.

**PREPARATION** None.

**PROCEDURE**

1 Start by establishing the meaning of the word *coma*. When you have done this explain that some hospitals are now using coma kits to help patients come out of a coma. Each kit consists of familiar and pleasing sounds, tastes and smells.

2 Ask each student to write down what they would want in their coma kit, e.g. a Liverpool football fan might find comfort in the song 'You'll never walk alone', a bird lover might want the sound of a nightingale, etc.

3 Ask them to show their piece of paper to another student and tell them to explain to each other the contents of their kit.

4 The students should be encouraged to move on to another partner periodically and the activity can continue as long as there is sufficient interest.

5 Round off the session by seeing if anyone found another student with a similar kit to their own.

## 51 How much energy do you have?

**LEVEL** **Intermediate and above**

**TIME** **30–40 minutes**

**AIM** To get a small group of students to explore their life style.

**PREPARATION** Make photocopies of the following task sheet for your class.

**TASK SHEET**

**Task 1**

Work individually to complete the following questionnaire:

| QUESTION **HOW MUCH ENERGY DO YOU HAVE?** ANSWER (tick your choice) | Frequently | Sometimes | Seldom or never |
|---|---|---|---|
| 1. Do you wake up feeling tired? | | | |
| 2. Are you too exhausted to go out in the evening? | | | |
| 3. Do you fall asleep in a chair watching TV or reading a book? | | | |
| 4. Do you smoke, drink coffee, or eat something sweet to give you an energy boost? | | | |
| 5. Do everyday activities such as shopping, housework, d-i-y, home maintenance, gardening, make your arms and legs tired? | | | |
| 6. Does tiredness affect your ability to think and concentrate? | | | |
| 7. Does fatigue make you irritable with your family and friends? | | | |
| 8. Do you long to have more energy? | | | |
| 9. Do your muscles ache at the end of a normal working day? | | | |
| 10. Do you find that your contemporaries have more stamina than you for certain tasks? | | | |

***Scoring:*** 2 points for every 'Seldom or never'
1 point for every 'Sometimes'
0 point for every 'Frequently'

***Energy rating:***
- High energy 17–20
- Moderate energy 13–16
- Average energy 9–12
- Below average energy 5–8
- Exceptionally low energy 0–4

When you have finished form a group with other students who have a similar energy rating. Your teacher will help you.

**Task 2**

Select one member of the group to act as secretary. Can you think of any reasons why your energy rating should be similar? Start by telling each other how you answered the questions. Did you give similar answers? When you have done this see if there are any similarities or differences between you as to:

- the number of hours you sleep every night;
- how active you are at work or school;
- the amount of exercise you take;
- the amount you eat and drink;
- your hobbies and pastimes;
- your age.

Would you like to have a higher energy rating? How would you achieve it? When you have finished ask the secretary to report on how you think people can raise their energy rating. See if the other groups agree or disagree.

**PROCEDURE**

1 Arouse interest in the discussion by getting students to think about health, fitness, etc. Advertisements for health food, etc. might be appropriate.

2 Give out the task sheet and give the students five or ten minutes to answer the questions individually. You may need to go through some of them.

3 Collect the scores from them and form groups of students with similar energy ratings.

4 Give the groups at least twenty minutes to complete Task 2.

5 Run a short feedback session where you ask the students to tell each other how to become more energetic.

## 52 Emotional match

**LEVEL** **Elementary and above**

**TIME** **20–25 minutes**

**AIM** To get students to talk about fears.

**PREPARATION** Make photocopies of the following task sheet for your class.

---

**TASK SHEET**

Answer the following questions by putting a tick (√) in the appropriate box:

| | | |
|---|---|---|
| Are you afraid of insects? | Yes □ | No □ |
| Are you afraid of the dark? | Yes □ | No □ |
| Are you afraid of death? | Yes □ | No □ |
| Are you afraid of flying? | Yes □ | No □ |
| Are you afraid of strange dogs? | Yes □ | No □ |
| Are you afraid of ghosts? | Yes □ | No □ |
| Do you become very nervous when you take exams? | Yes □ | No □ |

Join a group of five or six students and compare your answers to the questions. Is there anything you are all afraid of? Is there anything nobody is afraid of? Find out why people are afraid and help them if you can.

---



**PROCEDURE**

1 Tell the students that they are going to do a quiz to see what they are afraid of.

**2** Give out the task sheet and allow them about five minutes to complete the task on their own. Elementary students may need help with the vocabulary, and visuals may help.

**3** Set up the group work and give the students about ten minutes to discuss their answers. Make sure they try to make helpful suggestions.

**4** Get feedback from each of the groups.

## 53 Exchange

**LEVEL**

**Elementary and above**

**TIME**

**From 20 minutes upwards**

**AIM**

To encourage students to find out about each other by asking questions.

**PREPARATION**

None.

**PROCEDURE**

**1** Ask your students to take a large sheet of paper and write down the following:

**a. three dishes**
- your favourite dish;
- a dish you hate;
- the most unusual dish you have ever tried.

**b. three books**
- the first book you can remember reading;
- the name of the last book you read;
- the name of a book you will always remember.

**c. three places**
- your favourite holiday place;
- a place you really want to visit;
- a place you want to forget.

**d. three hobbies**
- something you enjoy doing;
- a hobby you want to start doing;
- a hobby you would never want to start.

**2** When they have done this, ask each student to find a partner he or she does not know well and exchange sheets. They should ask each other questions about any of the information that is of interest to them. Suggest a few questions such as these if necessary:
- *Why do you like . . .?*
- *What is . . .?*
- *Tell me about . . .*

They need not go through the whole sheet.

3 After about five minutes ask the students to change partners.

4 End the session by asking the students if they have found out anything interesting about the others in the group.

**REMARKS**

The technique can of course be adapted to any material but it should be used sparingly. Once or twice a year is enough.

## 54 Have you heard of . . .?

**LEVEL**

**Elementary and above**

**TIME**

**35–40 minutes**

**AIM**

To encourage cross-cultural exchange in mixed nationality groups.

**PREPARATION**

Make photocopies of the following task sheet for your class.

---

**TASK SHEET**

Think of three dishes and three famous places that represent a country that you know, but which you think the others will not know about. Now in four groups, labelled A, B, C, and D, share the lists of dishes and places you have made and decide which ones you think are the five most unusual dishes and places. When the group has agreed, write the new list on a piece of paper. Group A should exchange its list with group B. Group C should exchange its list with group D.

Stay in your original group and look at the list from the other group. Try and work out where you think the places are and where the dishes come from. Tell each other as much as you can about each one. If you really know nothing about these, invent an answer!

After about twenty minutes you should work with the group that gave you its list and tell each other your solutions. Which group got more answers correct?

---



**PROCEDURE**

1 Explain the nature of the task before giving out the task sheet.

2 Set up four groups (A, B, C, and D) as soon as the students have written their personal lists. Give the groups ten minutes to agree on a list of five unusual dishes and places.

3 Ask groups A and B to exchange lists, and groups C and D to exchange lists.

4 Give them up to twenty minutes to discuss the lists and work out their solution.

5 Get the groups who have exchanged lists, e.g. A and B, to meet to see who got the most answers right.

## 55 It's all in your hands

**LEVEL** **Upper intermediate to Advanced**

**TIME** **35–40 minutes**

**AIM** To get students to talk about personal characteristics, and discuss palmistry.

**PREPARATION** Make photocopies of the following task sheet, and also the illustrations and texts on pages 94/95.

---

**TASK SHEET**

Work with a partner you know reasonably well. Which of the following best describes the personality of your partner:

- energetic and self-confident;
- steady and systematic;
- sentimental and impulsive;
- creative with a strong imagination.

Tell your partner what you chose. Does he or she agree? Now look at your partner's hands and compare them to the illustrations your teacher will give you. Which hand does your partner's hand resemble? Is it a mixture of two or more of the hands illustrated? Which ones?

Now ask the teacher for the texts that accompany the illustrations. Make sure you understand all the adjectives that are used to describe people's personalities. If necessary use a dictionary to help you. Do any of the texts describe you or your partner? Do you have hands that match any of the descriptions? Do you think looking at people's hands is a clue to their personality?

Be ready to discuss the last question with the other members of your class.

---



**PROCEDURE**

1 Prepare for the discussion by finding out who believes in palmistry.

2 Ask each of your students to find a partner to work with who they know reasonably well.

**3** Give out copies of the task sheet and ask the students to read through it together.

**4** Be prepared to hand out the illustrations to each pair, and then the texts, when they are ready for them.

**5** When all the pairs have completed the task, bring the whole class together and run a feedback session. See if any of the doubters have changed their minds.

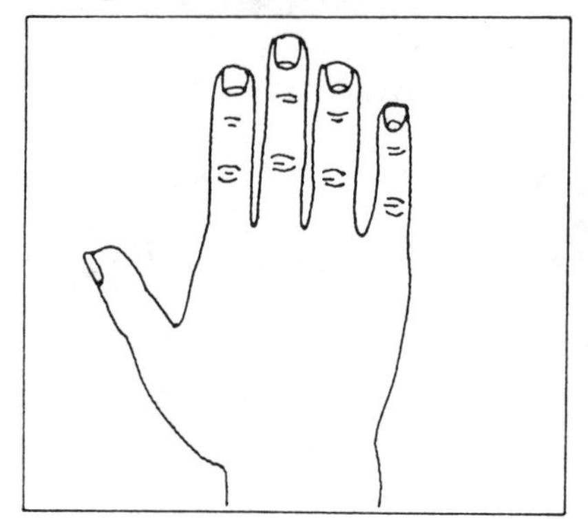

**The square hand**

**The spatulate hand**

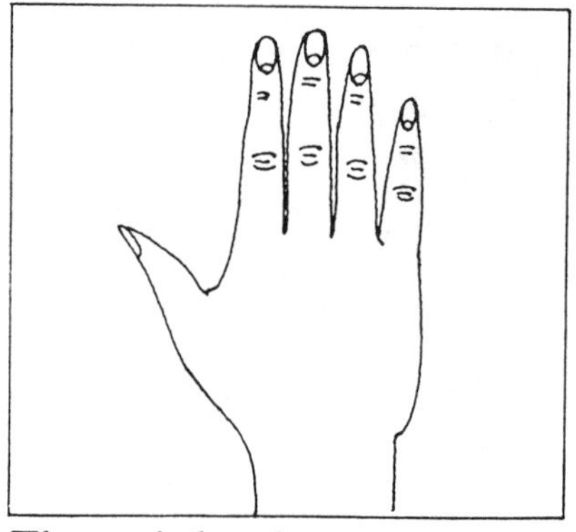

**The conic hand**

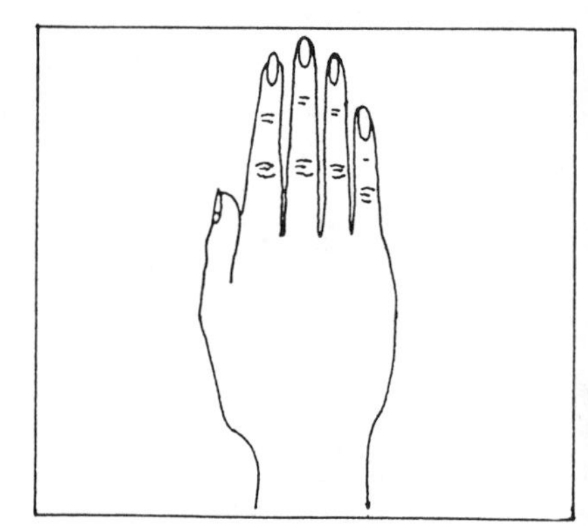

**The psychic hand**

## TEXTS

**The square hand**
The square hand is the hand of the organizer and planner. Owners of this hand love order, method and stability. They have a steady, systematic approach to life and they are not emotional by nature. People with square hands do not adapt easily to new circumstances. They are very careful with money. They make excellent engineers, doctors, and bureaucrats.

**The spatulate hand**
Spatulate hands are characterized by the 'fanning out' of the finger-tips in the form of a spatula. The best word to describe this form of hand is 'action'. People with spatulate hands are energetic, innovative, and self-confident. They are very practical and realistic. They are generally extroverts and very exciting to be with. Business, banking and construction are popular career areas for those with spatulate hands.

**The conic hand**
The conic hand narrows slightly at the fingertips. The skin texture is usually fine and this shows sensitivity and a love of beauty. People with conic hands are ruled by impulse and impressions. They are sentimental, intuitive and romantic. For them inconsistency is a big problem and they change frequently. They are very creative. If the hand is firm the creative energies are used for intellectual pursuits such as art or music. If the hand is soft, the person is very fond of rich food, money and comfort.

**The psychic hand**
The hand has long, graceful fingers with pointed tips. Like the conic hand the owners are very sensitive and they have an interest in beauty. People with psychic hands are motivated by their deepest feelings. They are very creative and have a strong imagination but they do not find it easy to deal with the practical problems in life and need strong friends.

Very few hands conform entirely to one of these types, and the mixed hand which contains aspects of two or more of them is in fact the most common.



# Ranking activities

In ranking activities students are required to put the items from a given list into an order of importance or preference. This rearranging phase is usually followed by a period of discussion when students explain or defend their choice. The material for ranking activities can be taken from a large variety of sources and adapted to the needs of particular groups of students. For example, students in a developing country might find it motivating to rank development projects or even professions in order of priority for their country. We could however in a more light-hearted exercise ask students to determine which of a list of professions would make the best husband or wife. These examples probe student attitudes, but there are ranking activities that rely more on common sense and general knowledge. One of the best known of these activities is the 'NASA survival game' in which students have to choose the most essential items to survive a 300 km trip on the moon. Variants on this one include desert or Arctic survival and usually even the most reluctant students can be drawn into the discussion. A standard procedure for ranking activities is as follows:

**1** Familiarize the students with the task through oral presentation. This should include arousing their interest as well as going through difficult vocabulary if necessary.

2 The students then work on their own and write down their solutions within a given time limit.

3 These lists are then compared in small groups or in the whole class. A pyramid discussion, in which groups of increasing size (two, then four, eight, etc.) discuss and agree on lists at each stage, is a popular variant.

Students need to realize that the most important stage is the discussion, which naturally practises the language for agreeing, comparing, contradicting, disagreeing, and giving reasons. The first of the activities presented is designed to introduce students to what is expected of them.

## 56 The best

**LEVEL** **Elementary to Lower intermediate**

**TIME** **20–25 minutes**

**AIM** To introduce students to ranking activities.

**PREPARATION** None.

**PROCEDURE**

1 Choose an area that your students are likely to be interested in, e.g. the cinemas in a particular town. Explain that they will rank the cinemas in their town from the best to the worst.

2 Decide on the criteria for distinguishing between good and bad cinemas. These can be elicited from the class, although some vocabulary will have to be supplied. Put a list of the criteria on the board, e.g. comfortable seats, good sound, etc.

3 Now make a list of the cinemas you want to evaluate. Tell the students they should then rank the cinemas individually before discussing their choice in groups or pairs. Elicit a few models to indicate that it is important to justify the decisions with sentences like, *Cinema X is the best because . . .*

4 Finally ask representatives to report to the class.

**REMARKS** Although cinemas may seem an unlikely topic this activity worked very well when it was used in a particular context overseas. The important thing is to choose something that all the students know something about. A variant which also worked well overseas was to give students a list of cars which were not manufactured in their country. Their task was to choose one that would be manufactured locally, and the same procedure as the one above was then followed.

## 57 Eureka!

**LEVEL** **Intermediate and above**

**TIME** **30–35 minutes**

**AIM** To promote discussion about inventions.

**PREPARATION** Put the following list of inventions in random order on a handout or OHT. Do not include the dates!

| | |
|---|---|
| Gunpowder | 1000 |
| Atomic bomb | 1945 |
| Wheel | 3000 B.C. |
| Screw | 200 B.C. |
| Paper | 105 |
| Printing | 1440 |
| Microscope | 1608 |
| Telephone | 1876 |
| Motor car | 1885 |
| Aeroplane | 1903 |

**PROCEDURE**

**1** Ask the students to work in pairs to decide on the approximate date for each of these inventions. When they have done this ask them to put the inventions in the order of their appearance, with the earliest inventions first. Allow them to check the answers with you.

**2** Now ask each pair to choose from the list three inventions that have had the most positive effect on civilization, as well as the three that had the most negative effect. They should discuss their choice with another pair and agree on a joint list.

**3** Finally, chair a feedback session in which each group presents its list. See if the class can come to a consensus.

**REMARKS** Students are likely to have different interpretations of the words 'positive' and 'negative'. This is worth exploiting, so allow them to settle the argument themselves.

## 58 Time

**LEVEL** **Intermediate to Advanced**

**TIME** **30–35 minutes**

**AIM** To get students to justify and explain their preferences.

**PREPARATION** Make photocopies of the following task sheet for your class.

**TASK SHEET**

Read the questions and answers below carefully. Number each of the answers 1, 2, 3, 4, or 5. Give 1 to the answer that applies to you most, 2 to the next, etc. Give 5 to the answer that applies least.

What would you do if you were given a year off work on full pay?

☐ Study for a further qualification in your field.

☐ Go on a trip round the world.

☐ Go and spend a long period of time in one or two countries you have always wanted to visit.

☐ Stay at home and use the free time to do things to your house.

☐ Use the time to earn extra money by doing another job.

How could you make better use of your time?

☐ By planning better.

☐ By getting things done faster.

☐ By wasting less time than you do at present.

☐ By finding more things to do.

☐ By relaxing more and not worrying about things.

Which of these would be your favourite time of year?

☐ A hot sunny day in the middle of summer.

☐ A cold clear day in winter.

☐ A frosty autumn morning with the leaves beginning to fall.

☐ A spring day with gentle rain.

☐ A sudden fall of snow in the winter.

Which of these is your favourite time of the day for working?

☐ Early in the morning.

☐ The middle of the day.

☐ The middle of the afternoon.

☐ The evening.

☐ Late at night.



**PROCEDURE**

**1** Give each student a copy of the task sheet and ask him or her to fill it in according to the instructions.

2 When they have finished ask them to share the results with a neighbour or a small group. Encourage the students to find out as much as they can about why the others completed the task in a particular way. They should aim to encourage each other to say more, rather than to argue.

3 End the session by checking on the degree of agreement within the different groups.

**REMARKS**

This technique can of course be adapted for use with questions about any topic.

# Value clarification tasks

Value clarification tasks are an extension of ranking activities and they serve to make people more aware of their attitudes and feelings. Value clarification techniques aim to get students to make explicit the reasons behind their judgement on a social issue, choice of a particular set of objects, etc. They follow a similar pattern to ranking activities in that a period of individual work is followed by group or class discussion. These tasks can be very threatening and they should not be introduced before a group has managed to get to know each other well, and have achieved a positive working relationship. The subject matter may also be unacceptable to students from some cultures, and teachers are encouraged to adapt these tasks if issues, such as sexual assault, are taboo.

## 59 Time capsule

**LEVEL**

**Intermediate to Advanced**

**TIME**

**25–35 minutes**

**AIM**

To encourage students to make explicit the things they value in their daily lives.

**PREPARATION**

None.

**PROCEDURE**

1 Explain to your students that they have to bury five objects in a time capsule which will represent everyday life today when it is opened in two hundred years time.

2 As soon as the students grasp the concept, ask each of them to prepare a list of five objects. There is no limitation as to size, weight, etc.

3 Divide the students into pairs, then fours, and then eights. At each stage they should reach a consensus about what should be included in the list of five objects.

**4** End the session by getting each group to report the details of their five objects to the rest of the class.

**REMARKS**

This is an activity that can be adapted to groups with special interests. For example, students of literature could be asked to choose three or five works to represent the literature of their country. The more personal the topic the more discussion it generates.

## 60 A just punishment

**LEVEL** **Upper Intermediate to Advanced**

**TIME** **30–35 minutes**

**AIM** To get students to consider the extent to which punishments fit the crime.

**PREPARATION** Make photocopies of the following sample letter for your class, or find other articles or letters in magazines which are more suited to your particular students.

---

**SAMPLE LETTER**

**A victim's verdict**
The man who sexually assaulted me has been sentenced to six months' imprisonment but will probably only serve four. My 'sentence' began on the night of the attack. I'm scared of walking anywhere alone. My parents are frantic with worry if I'm late. I have not been sleeping well, am prone to bursting into tears, and think constantly about the attack. Could I have done anything to ward him off? Why didn't I scream earlier? Was it my fault, even? These are questions I ask myself endlessly. I will probably serve my self-imposed sentence for the rest of my life. At present I am 16 years of age. I feel sickened by what I regard as a gross miscarriage of justice – even the maximum sentence for such an assault is only two years. It's extremely hard for anyone who has not experienced an assault of this kind to comprehend the feeling of devastation felt by the victim.

---



**PROCEDURE**

**1** Give out a copy of the letter to each student and ask them to read the text quietly on their own. Make dictionaries available if they require them.

2 When they have finished, ask them to write a word or sentence on a piece of paper, that summarizes their reaction to the letter. Collect all the pieces of paper and mix them up.

3 Ask each student to take a piece of paper and form a small group. Each student should then read what is on the piece of paper they collected so that the group can discuss the different reactions.

4 Ask each group to decide on the best way of punishing men who rape or sexually attack women. One member of each group should be ready to report their conclusions to the class.

**REMARKS**

This is not an activity to be used with an immature group. Sexual assault might be taboo in some cultures, but a similar technique can still be used with other content. For example, get students to react to 'The American Dream' text from *Speaking* (Elementary) in the Oxford Supplementary Skills series (1987).

## 61 Future shock

**LEVEL**

**Intermediate to Advanced**

**TIME**

**30–35 minutes**

**AIM**

To encourage students to discuss priorities for the future.

**PREPARATION**

Prepare the following statements as a handout and make photocopies, or write them on the blackboard or OHT.

---

**STATEMENTS**

By the year 2250 you will be able to:

- decide on the racial characteristics, IQ, sex, height, etc. of your baby;
- get specialist knowledge about any subject you want by dialling for the appropriate computer program;
- do all your shopping without stepping out of your home;
- achieve your ideal weight by taking an individual programme of diet pills and liquid food;
- prolong your life for up to fifty years if you go to special clinics for a period of two weeks a year after the age of forty;
- fly across the world in two hours in a low orbit spacecraft;
- decide not to work at all;
- get robots to do all the routine jobs in your home;
- take holidays in space;
- live in small communities rather than big cities, which will become more and more dangerous.

---

**PROCEDURE**

1 Set the scene by asking the students if they have considered what the world will be like in the year 2250.

2 After you get a few suggestions, explain that they are going to look at some of the predictions the futurologists have made for the year 2250. They should rank the developments by placing them in decreasing order of desirability, i.e. the developments they most want to see happen should come first.

3 When the students have completed their individual task, ask them to share their answers with a small group of three or four.

4 When everyone has given their views, the group should decide on three developments they think the world would be better without.

5 End the session by asking a member of each group to report to the rest of the class. See if the groups agree or disagree.

## 62 The bridge

**LEVEL** **Upper intermediate to Advanced**

**TIME** **30–35 minutes**

**AIM** A values task in which students decide on individual responsibility for a tragedy.

**PREPARATION** Make photocopies of the text opposite for your class, or find one more suited to your particular students.

**PROCEDURE**

1 Give a copy of the text to each student and ask them to read it carefully.

2 When they have finished, ask them to form groups of four or five and work together to complete the task.

3 Ask the students to write down the decreasing order of responsibility, and at the end run a pyramid discussion or a feedback session with the whole class.

**SAMPLE TEXT**

A young married woman, who was very lonely because her husband spent most of his time working, decided to take a lover. Her husband was on a business trip so she agreed to spend a night in her lover's house on the opposite bank of the river to where she lived. To get back to her house before her husband returned, she left at dawn the next morning and in order to reach home, she had to cross a bridge. Unfortunately there was a maniac on the bridge who threatened her, and refused to let her cross. She ran to a stranger to ask for help, but he refused to help her unless she gave him some money. She did not have any, and explained this to him, but the stranger refused to do anything unless he was paid in advance. The woman decided to go to her lover for money, but he refused and asked her to stay with him. She did not want to, so she went to see a childhood friend who lived near her lover. Her friend was a bachelor and had always declared his love for her, but she had never accepted him. She decided to tell him the whole story, and asked him for help. He refused to help her because he was disappointed in the way she had behaved. The woman went back to the bridge, and when the stranger still refused to help her, she decided to try to cross on her own. The maniac killed her.

Which of these people has most responsibility for her death: the woman, her husband, her lover, the stranger, her childhood friend, or the maniac?



**Acknowledgement**
This activity is similar to a task in *Challenge to Think* by Christine Frank, Mario Rinvolucri, and Marge Berer, (OUP 1982).

# Product orientated tasks

These tasks are characterized by the fact that students have to work collaboratively to carry out a set of instructions within a given time. The execution of the task involves students in the creative use of language. A subsequent follow-up stage, in which discussion can focus on the way in which the task was carried out, forms the basis for further practice.

# 63 From what I remember

**LEVEL** **Elementary and above**

**TIME** **20–25 minutes**

**AIM** For students to carry out and discuss the results of a simple memory experiment.

**PREPARATION** Decide on a coin you want the students to draw from memory. Make sure you have examples of the coin available for reference.

**PROCEDURE**

1 Divide your students into groups of five or six, and ask them to try to draw from memory exactly what is shown on each side of a coin they use frequently, for example, a fifty pence piece, if they are in England. The groups should all draw the same coin.

2 When all the students have finished, ask them to look at an example of the coin, and do the following:

- Find as many features of the coin as possible, e.g. identification, such as a head, the value, the date, etc.
- Find out who included the most features in his or her drawing.
- Find out who got the most features in the right place.
- Be ready to tell the other groups about their mistakes. Were they similar or quite different?

3 Tell your students that when this experiment was conducted in the United States, the people doing it could, on average, remember only three out of the eight features on the coin used. Often these were put in the wrong place.

4 Ask if the results in your students' groups were better or worse then those in the United States. Why? Ask them if they can suggest any reasons. Are they surprised at the results? Why? Why not?

# 64 A dream classroom

**LEVEL** **Elementary and above**

**TIME** **30–35 minutes**

**AIM** To get students to carry out a design task together.

**PREPARATION** Collect as many photographs as possible of early versions of typewriters, etc. as introductory material. Make photocopies of the following task sheet, or write the information on the blackboard or on an OHT.

**TASK SHEET**

Think of things that have changed in your lifetime. Can you remember anything from your childhood which you think is much better today? Tell each other about the changes and why you think it is better now. Now look at this statement:

> *Apart from the introduction of some audio-visual aids, classrooms have hardly changed at all in the twentieth century.*

Do you agree or disagree? Why?
Now work together and design a classroom for the twenty-first century. What would your classroom look like? What would it contain? How would it function?
Choose one member of your group to present your ideas to the class. When you have heard all the reports vote for the best classroom.



**PROCEDURE**

1 Start by establishing that the twentieth century has seen considerable changes. One way to do this might be to show your students photographs of early cars, etc. Once this has been established divide your students into small groups.

2 Give out copies of the task sheet and ask them to carry out the task.

3 Encourage your students to make interesting presentations.

# 65 Plan your time

**LEVEL** **Intermediate and above**

**TIME** **30–35 minutes**

**AIM** For students to consider ways in which they can learn English outside the classroom.

**PREPARATION** Make photocopies of the task sheet over the page for your class.

**PROCEDURE**

1 Arouse student interest in the planning task.

2 Set up the initial pair work and give the students five to ten minutes to discuss, add to or modify the list of suggestions.

3 When the initial discussion is over you should facilitate the setting up of groups. Allow the groups a maximum of twenty minutes to complete the planning task.

4 Chair the report back session in which each group presents its suggestions. Make OHTs or posters available to help the groups present their ideas.

**TASK SHEET**

Here is a list of techniques which people use to help them learn English outside the classroom:

- memorizing a list of words;
- reading a grammar book;
- doing grammar exercises;
- reading a book or a magazine in English;
- re-copying things from their class notebook;
- correcting mistakes made in written work;
- preparing the next unit of the coursebook.

Work with a partner and add any others of your own. Tell each other which ones in the list you find helpful, if any, then tell the class about the new ones you have added.
Arrange yourselves into groups and take a time period from this list:

- thirty minutes per day for six days a week;
- one hour a day for five days a week;
- two hours per day for four days a week.

In your group plan a programme to show how you could make use of the time to do extra work on your English. Use the ideas from the earlier list, as well as any others you can think of. Choose one person to present your plan to the rest of the class.



**REMARKS**

If students agree to experiment with a study plan, some time should be allotted in class for them to discuss how they are getting on.

## 66 My ideal phrase-book

**LEVEL**

**Elementary and above**

**TIME**

**35–40 minutes**

**AIM**

To get students to work together to produce and evaluate phrase-books.

**PREPARATION**

Collect together examples from phrase-books, including samples in the students' mother tongue, if possible.

**PROCEDURE**

**1** Start the lesson by dividing your students into small groups, and asking them the following questions:

- *Do any of you use phrase-books?*
- *Have you used them before?*
- *What do they usually contain?*
- *Do you find them useful? Why? Why not?*

2 Ask for a short report after a few minutes. During the feedback session suggest that the students' use of phrase-books might depend on the one they choose, and read them a few examples from nineteenth century phrase-books:

- My postillion has been struck by lightning.
- Where can we water our camels?
- My tailor is rich, etc.

3 Include some local examples if you can, and ask the students to discuss the examples.

4 Now ask the students to do one of the following tasks:

**a.** Decide on the headings for a phrase-book which the class would find particularly useful. Form small groups. Each group should then choose a section and write ten phrases for it.

**b.** Write part of a phrase-book to help people in your country understand English-speaking tourists.

5 Get the groups to report to the class when they have finished.

**REMARKS**

Very specific variants of the task can be devised, e.g. a group going on an excursion could draw up ten useful phrases. The important thing is to ensure that students find out whether their phrases are appropriate or not in the feedback session.

## 67 Building a model

**LEVEL**

**Intermediate and above**

**TIME**

**25–30 minutes**

**AIM**

For students to evaluate how effectively they are able to perform a given task.

**PREPARATION**

Construct a model from LEGO pieces. Provide enough LEGO pieces for four groups of students to construct the same model. (Provide extra pieces if you want to make the task more difficult.)

**PROCEDURE**

1 Divide the class into working groups of four. Give each group a collection of LEGO pieces and explain that they are to be used to build a model which is the same as the one in the next room.

2 Each group has to appoint an observer who can go and look at the model and report back to the group, so that they can build an exact copy of the model. The student who is the observer can go back and forth as many times as he or she wishes but should not 'build' at all. The task has to be completed in fifteen minutes and none of the other members of the group must see the model.

3 When they have finished, each group should work with the observer so as to prepare a report of the steps they took in

completing the task. They should also consider ways in which they might have done the task better. The report and the recommendations should be presented to the class for a general discussion.

**REMARKS**

It is very easy to do the task quickly if someone lays out the pieces while the observer draws a plan, etc. However the time constraint, as well as the interpersonal relations in the group, sometimes mean that a group will argue over procedural matters such as who should be the observer, rather than getting on with the task. Do not intervene, except to clarify instructions.

Obviously this task would work better with multilingual groups.

**Acknowledgement**
This has been adapted from a task we learnt from The Centre for British Teachers Ltd.

# Role plays

Role plays can range from highly directed and controlled activities, in which all the content is supplied to the students, to full-scale simulations in which participants determine what they will say on the basis of background information and the role they are given. (See *Role Play* by Gillian Porter Ladousse from the Resource Books for Teachers series (OUP, 1987).) The aim of this section is to present a few examples of role-play-type activities in which the students themselves have to use all their linguistic and non-linguistic resources in order to achieve their objectives in a loosely defined social situation.

## 68 I'll give you . . .

**LEVEL**

**Elementary and above**

**TIME**

**5–10 minutes** for one lesson, **20–25 minutes** for the next.

**AIM**

To set up a situation in which students buy and sell things.

**PREPARATION**

Make photocopies of the following task sheet for the two groups, and give the students prior warning before the class.

**TASK SHEET**

**Instructions for sellers**
Sellers should come to the lesson with five objects they wish to sell. These can be real things or pictures from magazines. None of the objects should be worth more than £50 or its equivalent. Imagine how much you paid for the objects and give your teacher a list of the prices. During the space of twenty minutes you should aim to sell each object for as much as you can get. Keep a note of each sale and, when the sale is over, tell the teacher how much money you have collected. Have you made a profit? The seller who makes the most profit is the winner.

**Instructions for buyers**
In this lesson the sellers will show you objects, or pictures of objects they wish to sell. You have a budget of £100 or its equivalent, and your aim is to buy as many objects as possible in about twenty minutes. You may need to bargain with the sellers to achieve your aim. When you have finished 'shopping', find out who was the best buyer and who was the best seller.



**PROCEDURE**

1 Set the task up by showing your students some examples of antiques. These can be photographs or actual objects. See if the students can guess the value of the objects.

2 After a brief discussion explain that the class will be split into two groups for a subsequent lesson. One group will be the 'buyers' and the other the 'sellers'.

3 Give them a copy of the instructions on the task sheet and agree on a time for the 'sale', which will take approximately twenty minutes.

# 69 Airport

**LEVEL** **Upper intermediate to Advanced**

**TIME** **30–35 minutes**

**AIM** To set up a conflict situation in which students have to decide what to do.

**PREPARATION** Make photocopies of the following task sheet for the different groups.

**TASK SHEET**

**Instructions for the ground staff**
You are in charge of a flight to Australia. The flight is due to close in twenty minutes. It is fully booked and none of the passengers at the desk have seats although they all have confirmed tickets. You expect there will be three seats available in about fifteen minutes, but you are not sure of this, and you do not want to tell the passengers in case there are none left. Until then you cannot accept luggage or give anyone a boarding card. Your aim is to calm the passengers down and get as many of them to accept £150 compensation in order to take another flight as soon as possible. The next available flight is in six hours' time, and you think there might be seats but you cannot check because the computer is not working. At the end of fifteen minutes you and your colleagues have to decide on which three passengers you will take. Find a way of telling the other passengers.

**Instructions for passengers**
You are booked on a flight to Australia. Decide on a role, e.g. a man or woman going to visit his or her relatives, a scientist speaking at a conference, etc. Approach the desk. Do not change your role. Try your best to get on the flight by talking to the staff and/or the other passengers.



**PROCEDURE**

**1** Set the task up with a brief general discussion about air travel. Find out if any of the class have ever been seriously delayed or overbooked. Ask them to recount what happened, how the different types of passengers reacted, etc.

**2** Now divide the class into passengers and ground staff. There should be one member of the airline staff for every three or four passengers. Once the students have been divided up, give each group its instructions.

**3** Monitor the role play.

**4** Follow up the task with an evaluation of how the various conflicts were handled or resolved.

# Discussion tasks

It can be very difficult to get students to talk unless their interest or imagination is stimulated. One common reason for failure is that students are expected to discuss complicated issues without much prior preparation or thought. One way to start students off is to give them some input. This can take a variety of forms, including sound tape, pictures, diagrams, a series of statements, texts, etc. The main consideration is that the input should not be so long or linguistically complicated that students focus on understanding it to the exclusion of any discussion.

## 70 Attitudes to gifts and giving

**LEVEL**

**Intermediate and above**

**TIME**

**25–30 minutes**

**AIM**

To set up a cross-cultural discussion about gifts and giving.

**PREPARATION**

Make photocopies of the task sheet over the page for the class.

**PROCEDURE**

**1** Orientate the students to the discussion.

**2** Divide your students into groups of four. Give each group a task sheet, and allow them twenty minutes to complete the task.

**3** When they have finished ask them to report on their discussion to the rest of the class.

**REMARKS**

British people would find some of these odd and attach much less importance to the etiquette of giving than many other races. Often the British will play down gifts, calling them, 'Just a little something . . .', and this can cause offence, as will the fairly normal practice of admiring other people's things. We believe that the practices on the list are observed to some extent by the following people:

- 1, 5, and 7 the Arabs;
- 3, 6, 9, and 10 the Chinese;
- 2 and 4 the Germans;
- 8, 9, and 10 the British and other Europeans.

**TASK SHEET**

Look at the statements below about giving and receiving gifts in different parts of the world, and decide which of the practices you:

- agree with;
- disagree with;
- find strange;
- would like to have in your country;
- think might be British.

**1** Only the right hand should be used for giving and receiving.

**2** When giving anyone flowers always give an odd number.

**3** When someone does anything special for you (even when it is part of their job) you should give them a present in return.

**4** Always take a gift for the hostess when you are invited to someone's house for an evening or for a meal.

**5** If your guest admires anything in your house you should give it to him or her.

**6** When it is their birthday older people are expected to give gifts of money in little red envelopes.

**7** You should say how good the present is as you hand it over. This shows how much you think of the person receiving the gift.

**8** When a couple plan to get married they make a list of the gifts they would like to receive as wedding presents.

**9** When you give a purse as a gift you should always put some money in it.

**10** If you give someone a knife, the receiver should pay you a small sum of money.

Now tell each other about any rules for giving and receiving gifts in your country.



## 71 Who's the boss?

**LEVEL** **Intermediate and above**

**TIME** **35–40 minutes**

**AIM** To discuss the role of secretaries at work.

**PREPARATION** Make photocopies of the following task sheet for the class.

**TASK SHEET**

Do you think good secretaries are indispensable to their bosses or not?

Now read the following extract about a senior executive who decides to work on his own.

> *HARD LINES: HOW THE BOSS WENT TO PIECES WITHOUT A SECRETARY*
>
> *'The business was there to be had, he found. It was the office side of things which bewildered him. For the first time in twenty-seven years he had no secretary to type his letters, answer his telephone, book his tickets, keep his diary, jog his memory, be polite to visitors and organise his papers. The room he called his study was awash with papers. His diary was always in the other pocket. The phone rang and no-one answered; he got an answering machine and forgot to turn it on. He misplaced letters and missed vital appointments. Typing was a disaster but his handwriting was worse and when the VAT inspector called he was almost prosecuted for evasion because no accounts had been kept at all.'*

Work in pairs and discuss the following questions:

- Do you think the story is exaggerated?
- Do you think it is true that the majority of bosses cannot function without their secretaries?
- Who make better secretaries, women or men? Or is the sex not important?

Now join another pair. Exchange your opinions about the previous and the following questions:

- Do you think more women should become bosses? Why? Why not?
- Do you think more men should be trained as secretaries? Why? Why not?
- Do you think it is right that secretaries are often paid much less than their bosses? Why? Why not?

After exchanging your views, make three concrete proposals for improving the situation of secretaries in your country. Report these to the rest of the class and see if they agree or disagree.



**PROCEDURE**

**1** Orientate the students to the discussion, e.g. by asking about the situation of secretaries in their country or company.

**2** Set up the pair work and give the students the task sheet. If necessary, help with the vocabulary of the text. When the students have read the text and have discussed the initial questions, you should set up the groups.

**3** Give the groups up to fifteen minutes to complete the discussion task. Make sure they know they have to report to the rest of the class.

**4** Chair a discussion in which the different groups get a chance to present their ideas. Remain neutral and avoid being drawn into the discussion. Guide the class to a consensus if at all possible.

## 72 Gifts

**LEVEL** **Elementary and above**

**TIME** **25–40 minutes**

**AIM** To encourage students to talk about gifts.

**PREPARATION** Collect together copies of selected extracts from mail order catalogues showing some unusual gifts such as a reversible watch, a heated cushion, etc. Make photocopies of the following task sheet for the class.

---

**TASK SHEET**

Choose a gift for yourself from the sheet your teacher has given you. Do not tell anyone what you have chosen. Now find a partner and choose a present for him or her. Exchange gifts and then compare what you chose for each other with what you chose for yourselves. Tell each other why you chose the two gifts.

Join another pair and find out what they chose from the list. Tell each other what you think of the gifts on the list. What sort of people buy them? Can you think of someone in the class to give each gift to? Give reasons for your choice. Come together as a class and compare your choices.

Finally, think of a gift that you have received that you particularly liked and one that you disliked. In a group of four tell each other about the gifts and what you did with them.

---



**PROCEDURE**

**1** Prepare for the task with a brief discussion about recent gifts, e.g. by showing students something you have just received.

**2** Give out the illustrations of the gifts and the task sheets, and give the students a few minutes to choose gifts for themselves and their partners.

**3** Give the pairs a few minutes to exchange gifts before joining another pair. Allow the groups of four up to ten minutes to select gifts for the class.

**4** Give the students a chance to distribute their gifts in a plenary session.

5 Ask the students to return to their group work in order to complete the rest of the task.

# 73 Love story

**LEVEL**

**Intermediate and above**

**TIME**

**40–45 minutes**

**AIM**

To use the plot of a well-known story as a stimulus for students to produce their own version.

**PREPARATION**

Make photocopies of the task sheet over the page for your class.

**PROCEDURE**

1 The task is in two parts. In the first part ask your students to reconstruct what they remember of the plot of a well-known film, e.g. *Love Story*. (Despite its age it is still being shown in many foreign countries.) If your students find it impossible to remember the story then read them a summary of the plot, which you will find below, before they go on to the main task.

2 Now go on to the second part of the task. Give each group of students a task sheet and ask them to complete it.

3 Be available to give help and advice if the students need it. Note any errors you had not previously anticipated for correction later.

**EXAMPLE SUMMARY**

Jenny Cavilleri (Ali MacGraw) is studying music at Radcliffe, a women's college in Cambridge, Massachussets. She meets Oliver Barrett (Ryan O'Neal) in the library. She is very rude to him but he asks her to go out with him. She goes to an ice-hockey match to see him play and they fall in love, even though she says the wrong things. Oliver meets Jenny's father who is a pastry cook who came to America from Italy. He likes Oliver but he does not get on with Oliver's father, who is very rich. Jenny and Oliver decide to get married. After their marriage Oliver's father refuses to support him in law school, and when Jenny graduates she has to work to allow Oliver to stay in college. Oliver graduates and gets a good job, but one day Jenny feels ill and she is taken to hospital. She dies. In the book the story ends with Oliver crying in his father's arms for the first time. In the film, Oliver's father comes to the hospital, but Oliver has nothing to say to him and they part.

**TASK SHEET**

Work in small groups. You are a team of people who have been asked to write the story for a new film aimed at the same audience that made *Love Story* a big hit when it appeared. The cast has not yet been named but the film company has a contract with four stars who usually appear as:

- a pretty young woman looking for the right man.
- an aggressive, but very handsome man, who has a bad reputation with everyone except for the women who love him.
- a devoted admirer who has everything a young woman should want, i.e. good looks, a little money, a good job, etc. but does not always get the girl because he is boring.
- an old lady who tries to have influence over everything and everybody.

Your story must include all of them in important roles. You have money in the budget for one more 'star' in addition to these four. Some of the typical ingredients for such a story include:

- a chance meeting;
- an inheritance;
- a serious illness;
- an accident.

but you can choose your own.

Each member of your group should present his or her ideas for the story. One of you should act as the secretary, and you should try to include all the group's ideas in a final story. Aim to have a 150 word summary of your group story by the end of the meeting.
Choose one student to present your story to the rest of the class.
Vote for the story that you think will make the most money.

# 5 Feedback

## Introduction

There are different ways of improving performance in language learning, but consistent and reliable feedback is a vital ingredient. Feedback can take different forms. For example, we can look at our own performance critically and try to improve through trial and error, or we can ask someone to help by analysing the performance and suggesting ways in which it can be improved. The latter is the basis of much sports coaching, and the principle can be applied to language teaching, and in particular the improvement of conversational competence. Unfortunately, however, the development and use of feedback techniques in the teaching of conversation is still a relatively neglected area. This may be because it is so complex. In conversation a variety of factors, including the speaker's accent, control of grammar and vocabulary, as well as overall fluency, all contribute to any impression of the performance. Consequently evaluation of the success or failure of conversational performance is not easy. In assessing oral competence we can, for example, say categorically that someone has failed to communicate effectively if they lack the linguistic resources to say anything at all. In cases where the student has apparently got his or her message across we may still be left with questions such as:

- Did the grammatical errors hinder communication or not? If not, do they matter?
- What effect did the student's accent, lack of fluency, etc. have on the listener? Would other listeners be more or less sympathetic? Does it matter?
- Was the information structured as efficiently or appropriately as possible? Does it matter?
- Was the message conveyed the one the student intended? How was it understood?

To allow this complexity to cause us to abandon any attempt at a systematic approach to feedback in the teaching of conversation, would be to abdicate responsibility, and the purpose of this chapter is to offer some practical suggestions in this area.

# What are feedback tasks?

The objective of feedback is to give students the information they need to improve on their performance. Areas for feedback in a programme aiming at the development of conversational skills include:

- grammar;
- appropriacy of vocabulary and expressions;
- fluency;
- pronunciation;
- non-linguistic factors affecting communication.

Feedback tasks aim to help the students look critically at their own performance in these areas with the help of observation sheets. Feedback tasks are similar to the awareness activities in Chapter 3, in that they too seek to raise the students' awareness of significant areas which affect conversational performance. They are nonetheless different, in that feedback tasks always use the students' own performance as the starting point.

# Preparing the ground

Feedback needs to be staged and selective if it is to avoid swamping and demoralizing the students. To achieve this teachers need to decide on the areas of conversational performance most relevant and important to their particular students. For example, a group of French waiters who are learning English might not be interested in losing an accent that is a major professional asset. Once the decision is made, it is a question of focusing on the chosen areas in turn until students reach the required performance level. To assist this process, teachers need to be continually aware of student performance and progress at any given point in the course. One way of doing this might be to keep a record card for each student. This can summarize how the students' performance in areas such as grammar, appropriacy, fluency, etc. combine in the performance of a particular task. An example of how such a card might look is given below.

| Name | Date | Nature of task (short talk, etc.) | Grammatical correctness | Appropriacy of vocabulary | Fluency and pronunciation | Overall performance |
|---|---|---|---|---|---|---|
| | | | | | | |

On this card teachers can record their impressions, as well as examples of specific strengths and weaknesses, so as to be able to direct the students to appropriate sources of help. A less time-consuming alternative would be to put these headings on a large sheet of paper and record general impressions of student performance.

## Using tape recorders

The use of tape recorders can play an important part in providing diagnostic information, and the recording of students during conversation lessons makes it much easier for the teacher to identify areas of weakness which can form the basis of subsequent lessons focusing on accuracy, the presentation of new language, etc. Other advantages of the use of tape recordings of students at work include:

- the opportunity for students to hear again their own performance and that of other students;
- the opportunity to look objectively at how students develop over a period of time. If you can obtain a recording of students at the beginning of the course this can be used as a basis for comparison at different stages of the course to illustrate progress. This can be important for confidence and morale when motivation begins to sag, since most people improve far more than they themselves realize.

If tape recorders are available it is worth encouraging students to record as much as they like so that they become unaware of the presence of the machine, but it is best to select only very short extracts to work on. These should usually be from the middle of a long recording. It is, on the whole, better to find extracts where several students are contributing unless the aim is to focus on a long turn.

The feedback tasks presented in this chapter were devised for use with tape recorders, but it is possible to adapt them for use in teaching situations where tape recorders are not freely available. (See pages 123–125)

## Training students to use feedback tasks

Students expect and require feedback. However, most students will equate feedback with the on-the-spot correction of error characteristic of controlled work. Consequently many students still feel that fluency activities are a waste of time because the teacher is not available to provide instant correction. It is very easy for them to lose confidence in themselves and the teacher if they feel consistently unsure that what they are doing is appropriate. The fact that correction is undesirable during fluency work does not always convince students, so feedback tasks can go a long way towards meeting a fundamental concern. However, it is important that students get a clear idea of how and why feedback tasks are to be used. Some learner training is therefore required.

The way in which the feedback tasks operate can be described to students with the help of the following diagram:

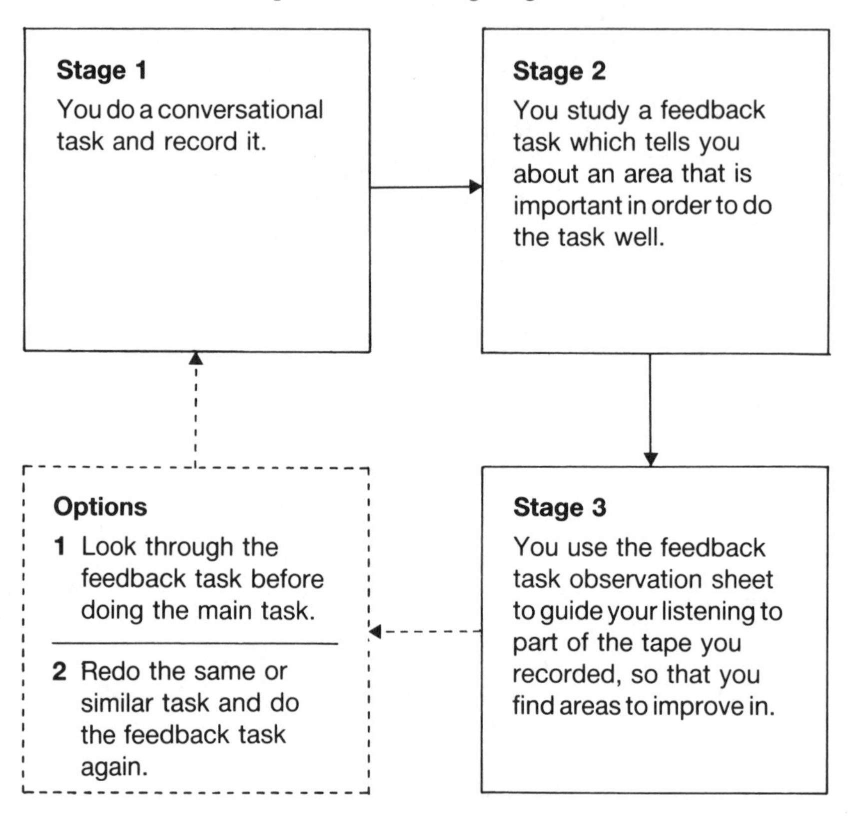


Many students will be unfamiliar with feedback tasks, so there is a value in taking the whole class through a task together before they work on their own. One of the initial tasks such as the one on pages 125/6, can be used with a piece of pre-recorded native or non-native speaker data, so that students develop a feel for how such tasks work. Give the students the feedback task to look at before playing the recording and try to elicit as many of the relevant points as possible, so that students know how the task operates.

The extent to which we can tell students why they are doing specific feedback tasks will depend on their level. However the general principle behind such tasks is readily accepted, even by elementary students. It is probably best to avoid jargon. Most students will be content with the explanation that these tasks will help them speak English like a native if they pay attention to their own performance and try to develop the appropriate verbal and non-verbal behaviour.

# Stages in setting up feedback tasks

**1** Decide on the area to be evaluated: this is a decision that is best left to the teacher initially. In time students may ask for feedback on areas that they perceive as weaknesses, and these should be incorporated if possible. Some tasks such as ranking activities, will naturally involve the language for agreeing, contradicting, giving reasons, disagreeing, etc. and each of these language areas can be the object of different feedback tasks. The important thing is to make sure that the area to be looked at in the feedback tasks would tend to occur naturally. It is best to base a decision about which task to use on the students' strengths and weaknesses.

**2** Set up conditions for the lesson: feedback is an important activity and it is therefore important to plan beforehand how feedback is to occur. Most of the feedback tasks in this section should really involve one tape recorder between every three or four students, although short talks or stories can be recorded in a language laboratory if one is available. Ideally there should never be too many students in one room as the noise from groups which are too close to each other has a disastrous effect on the quality of recordings and it is better if some students can move to another location. Cassette recorders with a sensitive in-built microphone which can run off a battery or the mains offer the greatest flexibility. The problem with external microphones is that they tend to provide a distraction and get knocked about. Built-in microphones will work quite well, as long as students sit in a tight circle.

**3** Prepare students for the recording: make one student responsible for the equipment in each group. This improves security and minimises disruption. Assuming that students know what feedback tasks are there are two possible approaches.

**a.** The first is simply to tell students to record themselves at a particular point of the task they are about to do. The objective of the recording then only becomes apparent when the feedback task is given out later.

**b.** The alternative is to tell students what is being focused on from the start. This could include discussing a tape or video model of the target performance and/or going through the feedback task first.

Some students react very positively to the second approach, but others become very self-conscious and refuse to say anything, so that the exercise becomes self-defeating. Modelling works best when students are involved with planned discourse such as short talks. It is probably best to see which approach suits particular groups better.

## The teacher's responsibility during the recording

The teacher should be available as a resource person during the recording session but should otherwise not interfere. It is wise however to monitor groups in order to see how they are getting on and, in cases where the teacher intends to go through the tape of a particular group, it is well worth making a few notes on the names of the participants, memorable phrases, etc. as these will help in the subsequent processing of the tape. Teachers may have to help students find a suitable part of the tape for exploitation.

## Using the feedback tasks in the book

The following is the procedure you might use.

**1** Give out copies of the task sheets.

**2** Take the students through the task sheet so that they know what to do. It is also very important that they know what they are looking for. Ways in which you might make this clear include:

- playing a short extract from one of the tapes the students will be working on;
- giving students a number of examples on the blackboard or OHP.

**3** Make sure that the students are seated around the cassette recorder so that they can all hear. Ideally students should listen to their own tape but form larger groups if this is impossible.

**4** Help the students find an appropriate section of the recording. In some cases you might have to listen to the tape before the lesson.

**5** Monitor the students as they carry out the feedback task and be ready to help if they require it.

**6** Get the students to report on their work. (See the next section.)

Students usually find that feedback tasks are difficult at the start but the benefits are enormous if they persevere. As they get used to using feedback tasks there will be less need to take them through each one.

## Feedback on feedback

A short period of time should always be built into feedback lessons so that students have the opportunity to give a quick report on what they have discovered while listening to the recordings. The session should be brisk and efficient and should concentrate on points the students feel are interesting or puzzling. The collection of recorded tapes, and in some cases completed tasks, can be used to monitor progress, as well as provide diagnostic information. In some cases the teacher may want to give students individual feedback on the tape which was made. In doing this it is important to ask the students to formulate their own judgements. This is essentially a process whereby the teacher tries to elicit what the students picked up from listening to the tape by asking them to describe their own performance. Once students are clear as to what happened, they are in a better position to see what they need to do in order to improve.

# Working without tape recorders

In teaching situations where tape recording is impossible or impractical, feedback tasks can still be carried out, although the process is less efficient. As always the first step is to decide on the area to be evaluated. If observation sheets are used to focus on an activity in 'real time', (i.e. as it occurs), it is particularly important to be clear about the feedback goals, so that observation is highly focused.

As soon as a decision is taken to look at a particular area, e.g. encouragement (Feedback task 4), the following options are available:

1 You can sit in with a particular group and use the task to monitor the group discussion yourself. It would be impractical to cover all the areas in the task, so you might limit yourself to looking for the presence or absence of the questions we use to encourage people to speak. A feedback session can be planned for later. This could be for the group itself, or the class as a whole, if general points emerge.

2 You can use the students as observers. One student could be appointed to be the observer for each group. In this case you would have to prepare an observer's sheet along the lines of the following example:

**Observer's task sheet**
Please read this handout carefully before you begin observing. If you have any problems, please ask. Do not allow any member of your group to read this handout.

You are going to observe the members of your group taking part in a discussion. Towards the end of the period of observation, place a tick (√) in the appropriate box (over the page) to record your general impression of the discussion.

| | Rarely | Sometimes | Almost always |
|---|---|---|---|
| **a.** The participants used expressions like *that's true*, *exactly*, etc. to indicate approval of what others said. | | | |
| **b.** They encouraged the others to continue by using *ah ha*, *mmmm*, etc. | | | |
| **c.** They smiled and nodded. | | | |
| **d.** They helped each other find the right words. | | | |
| **e.** They sounded encouraging. | | | |

Try to note down specific examples for **a.** and **d.** At the end of the group discussion ask the group for their own impression for each category. Lead a discussion in which the group agrees on ways in which they can be more encouraging. When you have finished present your ideas to the class.

It is very important that the observer's sheet indicates very clearly what students must do before, during, and after their period of observation. You could have more than one observer per group if you wanted to look at more than one area of performance (e.g. encouraging questions, as well as paralinguistic support). In this case assign the two areas to different students.

**3** It is also possible to give a group of students a simpler version of one of the feedback tasks in this book after they have finished an activity. They can then use what they remember of the task to carry it out.

The main problem of conducting feedback without using a tape recorder is the stress that this puts on the observer. It is also important that the observer is supportive. The role of observer should be to report and describe rather than evaluate. Discussion of the area chosen for feedback is generally sufficient for most students to formulate their own judgements. As the teacher, you may wish to make suggestions for improvement. If you do this, make sure that these suggestions are concrete and express them in terms of specific linguistic and paralinguistic behaviour (nod and smile more), rather than general advice (be nice!). Try to think through what you might say in advance, as students will expect some comment.

# Feedback tasks

The tasks which follow fall into one or both of the following categories.

**Category 1**
In these the students are asked to note the presence or absence of particular features on the basis of examples given.

**Category 2**
Students are asked to note down what was said or done to achieve a particular interactional aim. The notes can then be used to compare their own performance with what a native speaker or high level non-native speaker might do in a similar communicative setting. Generally speaking, the first group of tasks are easier and should therefore be used first.

The tasks in this chapter focus on some of the most important features of native speaker conversation. Readers are encouraged to write their own feedback tasks on the basis of the examples provided if they wish to focus on any specialized areas which are not covered. The tasks can also be adapted for use with different levels by altering the length of the task as well as the complexity of the instructions.

## Feedback task 1

**LEVEL** **Elementary to Advanced** (adapt to the needs of a particular level).

**AIM** For students to look closely at the language they use.

**USE** Suitable for use with any task.

**PREPARATION** Make photocopies of the following task sheet for the class.

**TASK SHEET**

**1** Choose a two minute extract of the recording you have just made and listen to it in your groups.

**2** Choose one of these areas each and make a note of any errors that were made in:

- the verb tenses used;
- the nouns used;
- the adjectives used.

When you do this, listen for pronunciation errors, as well as problems of meaning or grammatical form, (e.g. *she walk* instead of *she walks*).

**3** Discuss your notes with the other members of the group. Work out a correct way of saying the same thing. Ask the teacher for help if none of you knows the answer.



**PROCEDURE**

See notes on page 122 before dividing the students into groups of three or four.

**REMARKS**

A variation of this type of task can be used throughout a course. It is important that students realize that there are different types of errors, and teachers should provide a few illustrations at the start. In cases where a task would be expected to throw up certain tense forms or vocabulary items, the students could be directed to listen for examples of these. It would also be useful to have reference material, such as *Practical English Usage* by Michael Swan (1980), so that students can be encouraged to solve their own problems.

# Feedback task 2

**LEVEL**

**Elementary to Advanced** (adapt to the needs of a particular level).

**AIM**

To focus on encouraging expressions.

**USE**

Suitable with tasks in which students share personal information.

**PREPARATION**

Make photocopies of the following task sheet for the class.

**TASK SHEET**

**1** Select about two minutes from the recording of your discussion with your group or partner.

**2** Listen to your recording and see if you can find examples of the following:

**a.** Expressions like:
- *Really?*
- *Is that right?*
- *That's nice/interesting/unusual*, etc.
- *It sounds interesting/lovely/fascinating*, etc.

**b.** Questions that repeat a key word from what the other person has said. For example:

**A** I usually go windsurfing.
**B** *Windsurfing?*
**A** Yes, I go . . .

or

**A** What's the weather like in Morocco?
**B** Not too bad, but it often rains.
**A** *Rains!*
**B** Oh yes, I'm afraid so, but . . .

These expressions encourage the other person to say more. Try introducing these into your conversation.



**PROCEDURE**

Follow the procedure on page 122 before allowing your students to listen to their own tape in pairs or small groups.

**REMARKS**

It is worth practising the intonation (usually a rise) so that students sound interested when they use these expressions. Nodding and smiling will also help them to look interested. All these strategies will generate a lot of useful input for students.

## Feedback task 3

**LEVEL**

**Elementary to Advanced** (adapt to the needs of a particular level).

**AIM**

To focus on fillers and hesitation devices.

**USE**

Suitable with any task that produces examples of connected speech, e.g. the telling of an anecdote.

**PREPARATION**

Make photocopies of the following task sheet for the class.

---

**TASK SHEET**

1 Work with a partner. Make a recording of each of you telling a short story.

2 Listen to the tape once. Do you think the story sounded natural or not? Why? Why not?

3 Now listen to the extract again. Can you notice the following:

a. Noises such as *erm*, *mmm*, and *err*.
b. Phrases such as *well*, *so then*, *anyway*, *Oh and*, etc.
c. Phrases that involve the listener in the story, such as *you see*, *you know*, *do you see what I mean?*, etc.

All of these help to make you sound more natural, and native speakers use them all the time. See if you notice some of them next time you hear a native speaker talking.

Discuss what you have noticed with your partner and decide how and where the recordings you made could be improved. Finally, listen to the two stories again and tell each other what you liked best about the other person's story.

---



**PROCEDURE**

Follow the procedure on page 122 before asking the students to listen to their own tape in pairs. Set up small groups if there are insufficient machines.

## Feedback task 4

**LEVEL**

**Elementary to Advanced** (adapt to the needs of a particular level).

**AIM**

To focus on the strategies we use to keep a conversation going.

**USE**

Suitable with tasks where students have to exchange personal information or chat.

**PREPARATION**

Make photocopies of the following task sheet for the class.

**TASK SHEET**

**1** Make a recording of your group discussion.

**2** Choose a two or three minute section of your cassette where most people in the group had something to say. Listen in particular for any examples of questions people asked to encourage the speakers to say more about themselves, e.g.

- *So what did you do then?*
- *And did that work?*
- *Do you think you'd do it again?*
- *When did it all happen?*
- *Why did you decide to . . .?*
- *How did it happen?*

Write down examples of any questions you hear and discuss them in your group, and then answer the following:

**a.** Were they grammatically correct?
**b.** Were they suitable? (i.e. not too personal).
**c.** Did they help the conversation go forward?
**d.** How could you improve the questions?

**3** Now listen for places in the conversation where there was a break or a silence, (e.g. where nobody knew what to say next). Discuss these breaks in your group. Were they natural and acceptable? If not, how could you make the conversation develop more easily? A question? Showing interest? Asking another person's opinion?

Discuss how you would improve the conversation.



**PROCEDURE**

Set up small groups after you have been through the procedure on page 122. Check that the groups are working on an appropriate section of the tape.

## Feedback task 5

**LEVEL**

**Elementary to Advanced** (adapt to the needs of a particular level).

**AIM**

To focus on story telling devices.

**USE**

Suitable with tasks in which students tell a story.

**PREPARATION** Make photocopies of the following task sheet for the class.

---

**TASK SHEET**

1 Work in small groups and listen to one of the stories you have just recorded with the following questions in mind:

a. Did the story start with an expression to get the listener's attention?
b. Did the story-teller talk at the same speed all the time? Did the story-teller's voice go faster or slower at any point? When? Were these changes connected to the meaning of the story?
c. Did the story-teller use his or her voice to make the story more exciting or dramatic? How?
d. Were certain words stressed more than others to hold the listener's attention? Which ones?
e. Was the ending of the story clear? How did you know it was the end?

2 Now listen to the story again. Which parts did you enjoy? Which parts could you improve? Discuss how you could make the story more interesting. Use the questions in the first part of the task to help you make suggestions. If you have time, make a second recording.

---



**PROCEDURE** Follow the procedure on page 122. Note that the students will probably need some input on story telling devices in English, and it may be worth listening to a well told story with the help of the questions for the first part of the task. Ideally this should be in English, but a story in the students' own language would help make the point. Teach formulae such as *Once upon a time*, as appropriate.

## Feedback task 6

**LEVEL** **Elementary to Advanced** (adapt to the needs of a particular level).

**AIM** To focus on how we make and respond to suggestions in order to encourage people to be constructive.

**USE** Suitable with any task where students have to work collaboratively.

**PREPARATION** Make photocopies of the following task sheet for the class.

**TASK SHEET**

**1** Make a recording of your group as it works to complete the task your teacher has set you.

**2** Choose a four or five minute section of your cassette when most people had something to say.

**3** Listen for the ways in which people made suggestions. Were any of the following used?

- *Why don't we . . .?*
- *We could . . .*
- *I know . . .*
- *How about . . .?*

Write down any others that you hear. Discuss in your group whether the suggestions were grammatically correct and if they could be improved.

**4** Listen to the tape again and note how people responded to the suggestions. Did they use any of the following expressions?

- *Yes, that's a good idea.*
- *Yes, and then we could . . .*
- *That's a nice idea, but I don't think . . .*
- *Do you think it would work?*

Write down any others that you hear.

**5** Decide in your group:

**a.** Do the responses build on what the person has said?
**b.** Do they encourage other people to speak?
**c.** Do they stop the conversation?

If they stop the conversation, decide how they could be improved. When we work together to produce something, it is important that we show we are listening carefully to others and that we try to respond positively to what they say, even if we then change the idea.



**PROCEDURE**

Take your students through the procedure on page 122. Make sure they are listening to an appropriate section of their tape.

## Feedback task 7

**LEVEL**

**Elementary to Advanced** (adapt to the needs of a particular level).

**AIM**

To focus on the ways in which we seek and give opinions.

**USE**

Suitable with any task in which students are likely to give their opinions freely. Ranking or value clarification tasks usually generate lots of examples.

**PREPARATION**

Make photocopies of the following task sheet for the class.

---

**TASK SHEET**

1 Make a recording of your group taking part in a discussion.

2 Choose a short section of your recorded discussion where everyone in your group had something to say. Listen in particular for the ways in which people introduced their own opinions. For example, can you hear any examples of the following:

- *I think . . .*
- *Well, in my opinion . . .*
- *I believe . . .*
- *As far as I'm concerned . . .*
- *Well, in my country . . .*

Write down all the other examples you hear.

3 Discuss in your groups:

**a.** Whether the expressions used to give opinions were grammatically correct or not. Ask your teacher for help if necessary.

**b.** Do you think that the expressions are used too often in your discussion? Are people listening to each other enough? Or do they sound as though they are only interested in their own opinions? Discuss possible improvements.

4 Listen to the tape again. Are there any examples of asking for other people's opinions? Can you hear any examples of the following:

- *What do you think, X?*
- *Do you agree?*
- *What's your view?*
- *Is it like that in your country?*

Expressions like these involve the other speakers in the discussion and help to make it more fluent and interesting. When you have made a list of examples from your recording, go on to do the following:

**a.** Discuss with the group whether they were grammatically correct and how you might improve any that were wrong.

**b.** Decide where more examples of asking for other people's opinions could have been included.

---



**PROCEDURE**

Follow the procedure on page 122. Make sure your students are listening to an appropriate section of the tape.

# Feedback task 8

**LEVEL**

**Elementary to Advanced** (adapt to the needs of a particular level).

**AIM**

To focus on ways of introducing polite disagreement.

**USE**

Suitable with any task where disagreement is likely.

**PREPARATION**

Make photocopies of the following task sheet for your class.

---

**TASK SHEET**

**1** Make a recording of your group discussion.

**2** Choose a two or three minute section in the middle of your discussion where most people in the group had something to say. Listen in particular to the point where one speaker takes over from another. Note down what they say to show that they were listening carefully to the previous person, before adding their own opinion. For example, do they use expressions like:

- *That's an interesting idea/point.*
- *Yes, I think that's right.*
- *Do you really think so?*

**3** Listen for points where the change from one person to another sounds sharp or impolite, and discuss with your group how it could be improved.

**4** Listen to your cassette again and note down any examples of language that shows the attitude of the speaker to what he or she has heard, e.g. agreement or disagreement. Particularly where there is disagreement, does the speaker sound abrupt, aggressive or impolite? If so, why? Would any of the following expressions help to make the discussion sound more friendly?

- *Erm, well, I'm not sure about that. Perhaps . . .*
- *I can see why you think that, but . . .*
- *No, I'm sorry, I don't think that's really true.*
- *Yes, but . . .*
- *I know it's difficult, but . . .*
- *Don't you think . . .?*

Discuss with your group how the discussion could be improved.

---



**PROCEDURE**

Follow the procedure on page 122. Make sure your students are listening to an appropriate section of the tape.

# Feedback task 9

**LEVEL** **Elementary to Advanced** (adapt to the needs of a particular level).

**AIM** To focus on giving a talk.

**USE** Suitable with any pre-prepared talk aiming at giving information.

**PREPARATION** Make photocopies of the following task sheet for your class.

---

**TASK SHEET**

1 Listen to the recording of a talk prepared by another group.

2 During the first listening answer the following questions as you listen:

**a.** Does the talk sound interesting?
**b.** Does it sound fluent?
**c.** Is it easy to understand?

If the answer to any of the questions is 'no' or 'it could be better', try to decide why. These questions might help you. Discuss them in your group.

**a.** Are there too many breaks and hesitations?
**b.** Is the voice too flat?
**c.** Is the pronunciation and stress difficult to understand?
**d.** Does the speaker say and do enough to hold the listeners' attention?
**e.** Is the information presented in an order that is easy to follow?

Try to find examples on the cassette to support your decisions, and discuss how you could improve the talk. Ask your teacher for help if necessary.

3 When we give this kind of talk it is important that it has a clear beginning, middle and end. This helps us to follow and understand what the talk is about. Listen to the talk again and decide which section is the introduction, which section gives the main information, and which is the conclusion. How did you decide? Write down the words and phrases that helped to tell you. Did you hear any of the following?

In the introduction:
- *The topic of my talk is . . .*
- *I'd like to begin by . . .*
- *I shall divide my talk into X parts.*
- *First of all I'd like to . . .*
- *As an introduction to my talk . . .*

In the main body of information:
- *Firstly, . . .*
- *Secondly, . . .*
- *The advantage of . . .*
- *The disadvantage of . . .*
- *The most important thing to remember is . . .*

In the conclusion:
- *I'd like to finish/conclude/summarize by . . .*
- *Let's go through the main points again, . . .*
- *I hope that what I have said will . . .*

If necessary discuss how the talk could be made clearer.

**4** Listen to the talk a third time and pick out examples where you thought the speaker did well. Get together with the students who recorded the talk and tell them about your discussions.

---



**PROCEDURE**

Follow the procedure on page 122. It may be worth taking the students through an example of a good talk at some stage.

## Feedback task 10

**LEVEL**

**Elementary to Advanced** (adapt to the needs of a particular level).

**AIM**

To focus on how we use communication strategies to carry on speaking.

**USE**

Suitable with any discussion.

**PREPARATION**

Make photocopies of the task sheet over the page for your class.

**PROCEDURE**

Follow the procedure on page 122.

**TASK SHEET**

Listen to the recording you have just made. Did any of your group have trouble finding the right words at any point of the discussion? When? What happened? Discuss the following:

**a.** Did another speaker take over?
**b.** Did the others help you by giving you time to think?
**c.** Did another speaker help you by giving you the words you needed?
**d.** Did you use a word that was similar in meaning to the one you wanted, e.g. the word 'shop' instead of 'department store'?
**e.** Did you invent a new word?
**f.** Did you paraphrase or describe the thing you didn't know the word for? For example, 'a bus that takes tourists' rather than 'a coach'.
**g.** Did you use your hands to describe what you were trying to say?
**h.** Did you use a word from your own language?
**i.** Did you do something else? What?

Inventing words, paraphrasing, using your hands, etc. are all examples of communication strategies, and good communicators use these to keep talking.

Could you have used any of these strategies at any point of the recording? When we have trouble finding our words we often lose our chance to speak. Using communication strategies can help us to avoid this.



# Direct feedback

Although the use of feedback tasks reduces student anxiety about correction, students will continue to expect the teacher to give them direct feedback on their performance. A full treatment of error is beyond the scope of this book. However, a few general points can be made.

In first language acquisition, mothers often indicate approval of a child's communicatively appropriate but badly formed utterance prior to expanding or modifying it. For example:

**Child** Daddy go supermarket.
**Mother** Yes. Daddy's gone to the supermarket.

This is a technique which is used by some language teachers today, and although it does not highlight the source of the error at all, it can be a useful technique to adopt when the focus is on fluency.

Many students find it very threatening to speak a foreign language in public, and this form of correction will tend to encourage students to take risks because it is less inhibiting than more overt correction techniques.

In conversation teaching teachers should always aim at minimal intervention during fluency activities. This means getting students used to delayed feedback so that, again, they feel at ease talking at length and taking risks. Error treatment can then occur at a later date or time, as long as it is not left for more than a week.

## Post-lesson error treatment

There are a number of ways in which this can be organized. One way would be for the teacher to try to make notes of errors which occur during group work. Teachers should be clear about what they are concentrating on, (e.g. verb forms). Using a grid or checklist can help to focus the attention and makes the task easier. The notes can then form the basis of a subsequent discussion. The main reason for not leaving error treatment for too long is that it is important that students can still remember the context in which the error was made. Teachers should also make sure that the notes are of interest to other students by focusing on points of general interest. The main trap to avoid is merely telling the students what they should have said. A combination of these tasks might be used to avoid this happening:

- Put up a list of utterances which occurred during the conversation and ask students to decide whether they are correct or not.
- Ask students to decide whether the utterances were appropriate or not in the context in which they occurred.
- Ask students to decide whether certain pronunciations were correct or not.
- Put up a list of incorrect forms and ask students to correct them.
- Ask students to work out the correct pronunciation of words on the board.
- Ask students to work out a range of appropriate alternatives for words or expressions used at certain points of the conversation.
- Ask students to use expressions which were correct, but inappropriate, in a more appropriate context.

Essentially this is a process whereby students are being given information on which they can base a subsequent performance, but the general principle we favour is to try to ensure that students are able to perceive where the error lies by making an effort to find the right form. It goes without saying that answers must be made available, although there is no reason why reference books should not be used so that students can try to solve their own problems. Comments should always be elicited from the students themselves first.

An alternative to pencil and paper work is to base post-lesson error feedback on a recorded extract of one of the group tasks. The procedure is for the teacher to listen carefully to the extract, with a view to selecting a very short section for exploitation. The teacher should then aim to transcribe the tape. It is very difficult to note down exactly what is on a tape and for teaching purposes it is not important to aim at 100 per cent accuracy. However, teachers should avoid the temptation to regularize what was said, since hesitations, false starts, etc. are perfectly natural. The transcription can then be given to students, so that they can read it while listening to the tape. They can then work out the errors and correct them, and the teacher can drill and practise the correct forms as required. Transcripts take a long time to prepare and work through properly, so a page or two provides plenty of material. Transcripts of tape-recorded extracts are widely used in *Community Language Learning*, and readers might wish to consult an account of this for further ideas in this area, (e.g. Rod Bolitho in *Practical English Teaching*, March 1983). It is possible to get students to listen to the extract without a transcript. If this is done it needs to be highly directed, as it will be very difficult for anyone to get more than a few words down (with the possible exception of the students who made the original recording). The quality of home recordings is usually not very good so a transcript should be used at some point, in order to ensure students do not become frustrated and bored. Remember, never to be entirely negative and use these sessions to bring out positive features of the students' performance as well.

In general then the teacher should aim to:

**1** Encourage students to formulate their own judgements wherever possible.

**2** Be constructive and encouraging. Mention good things as well as bad, and always make concrete suggestions for improvement.

**3** Help students to see why they have succeeded or failed.

**4** Focus on a few things of interest to everyone and deal with very individual problems separately.

# Video-based feedback

The increasing availability of video cameras has meant that it is possible to use video recordings as a basis for feedback. When video is used to record presentations or talks, students often try harder, since television is still a medium which has some novelty value. However it can be very difficult to get good film of natural small group interaction outside a studio with only one camera, and in this respect video has its limitations. The main advantage of video-based feedback is that it allows for the possibility of focus on paralinguistic areas, such as the use of gesture, facial expression, etc. which can be so important in communication. Areas to look out for include:

1 Hand movement – speakers who wave their hands around in an uncoordinated way distract from the message. At the same time, good speakers will use their hands to reinforce a point.

2 The speaker's gaze – it is very disconcerting to listen to someone whose eyes are fixed on the floor or the ceiling. Speakers should try to make eye contact with the people they are talking to.

3 The speaker's facial expression and its suitability for the message.

4 Body language – persistent swaying or fidgeting is very distracting. We tend to show interest by leaning forward in the direction of the person we are talking to. Smiling and nodding, as well as making encouraging noises, will give the impression we are listening and make the other person well disposed towards us. It is important for non-native speakers to look interested if they want native speakers to talk to them.

The feedback tasks mentioned earlier can also be used on video recordings of students.

For classroom purposes, the rule must be that any of the areas mentioned above should only be a source for comment when the teacher is confident that it is possible to make concrete suggestions for improvement. For example, some speakers deal with the problems of excessive hand movement by putting a free hand in a pocket or hiding their hands from view of the people they are talking to. Suggestions such as this are relatively easy for the students to follow. However, comments such as, *You've got a silly expression* should always be avoided. They are unhelpful and will tend to inhibit students even if we subsequently follow them up with positive suggestions. Our self-image is very important to us, and this is an area where we should always tread carefully. As always, it is better to get student reaction first, and if students fail to realize what they look like to others, it may not be worth pursuing it. This is a specialized area, so it is important that people develop their own personal style. Limit discussion to areas where it is possible to give simple direct advice. Finally, some students can be very self-critical, and it is therefore very important to be positive as often as possible.

## Feedback on the group process

All the feedback tasks we have looked at to date have concentrated on what people say. However, a lot of conversation work occurs in groups, so it is worth reflecting on how efficiently and effectively students are able to work in groups.

The advantages of group work include:

- an increase in the quantity and quality of the interaction between students;
- the development of interpersonal skills;
- an opportunity for student autonomy and responsibility;
- an opportunity to accommodate a variety of learning styles and strategies.

Although these advantages are widely accepted, teachers should never lose sight of the fact that working with others can be a stressful experience. There is always a potential for conflict. One or more of the students may try to dominate a group. Antagonism or withdrawal can quickly build up, and working with others can be a threat. Although teachers should avoid becoming amateur group therapists or psychoanalysts, a watchful eye on the roles that students adopt in group work can be helpful. Some of the main types of role are as follows:

**Leader** — someone who tries to direct and control the group, maybe in a dominating or insistent fashion.

**Harmonizer** — someone who tries to keep things going by making positive comments and encouraging others.

**Blocker** — someone who continually seeks to criticize or resist what other people say.

**Avoider** — someone who tries to be non-committal and who is content to follow others to the point of not contributing at all.

The risk is clearly that dominant or negative members of a group provoke withdrawal or discontent. A certain amount of conflict is inevitable and natural as people get used to working with each other. However, tensions can persist or develop to the extent that the learning is hindered. When this happens, it is usually apparent, but there is no instant solution. Sometimes a change in the composition of a group works wonders. Sometimes the teacher has to speak to the people involved. Perhaps the best thing is to encourage students to talk to each other about the way they took part in particular tasks so that students become aware of the way in which their behaviour may be affecting others. If this is done a lot of problems simply do not reach crisis point. We can do this through special tasks, such as the ones which follow, or more simply by putting up the following type of instruction at the end of a period:

*Spend five minutes discussing how you might have done the task more quickly and efficiently.*

The important thing is to encourage students to see that group work is a collaborative activity, so that if they co-operate, everyone benefits.

**Acknowledgement**
Mike Breen of the University of Lancaster encouraged us to think about the group process.

## Feedback task 11

**LEVEL** **Upper intermediate and above**

**AIM** For students to consider how they behave in meetings.

**PREPARATION** Make photocopies of the following task sheet for the class.

---

**TASK SHEET**

| Moves | Frequency |
|---|---|
| **1** Seeking information | |
| **2** Giving information | |
| **3** Suggesting/originating | |
| **4** Positive reaction:<br>– building/adding<br>– supporting/personally friendly | |
| **5** Negative reaction:<br>– blocking/objecting<br>– attacking/personally hostile | |
| **6** Summarizing/guiding | |

---

## PROCEDURE

**1** The task sheet is an observation grid. The things we say in meetings can be identified as falling into a very simple range of behaviours or moves. The objective is to identify each contribution a participant makes, so that a picture of what people did in a meeting can be built up. So in this short example:

**A** What about production Tom?
**B** Well, we're dealing with urgent orders now but we should be able to start on the new project soon.
**A** Well, we could work overtime.

Student A seeks information and suggests something, so his or her sheet would be marked twice, in the following way:

| **Moves** | **Frequency** |
|---|---|
| **1** Seeking information | ✓ |
| **2** Giving information | |
| **3** Suggesting/originating, | ✓ |
| etc. | |

Student B's sheet (not illustrated) would be marked once in box 2, (giving information).

**2** Show your students how the system works by going through a short transcript of a meeting. Once they understand the system it can be used in the following ways:

**a.** Students can go through a recording of a meeting or discussion in order to focus on the contributions made by the participants.
**b.** Observers can use the sheet to look at how selected individuals perform during a meeting.

The following points might emerge in a discussion of the results of an observation:

- negative or blocking behaviour inhibits group discussion and makes participants antagonistic to the originator;
- building contributes to a very positive impression of the person who does this regularly;
- someone who is prepared to give ideas and make suggestions is considered a valuable member of any group;
- chairpersons and group leaders should seek information far more than they give it (up to eight times more often is considered appropriate).

**3** If you are lucky enough to have several students in your class who are prepared to give ideas and make suggestions these are valuable members. You should therefore spread them around. However, if there is no one prepared to do this some form of outside input will be needed.

**4** Once your students get a feel of how they are behaving, they can attempt specific goals, e.g. increasing the number of positive remarks they make in a discussion.

**Acknowledgement**
The list in the task sheet is based on work discussed in *Developing Interactive Skills* by Neil Rackham, (Wellens Publishing, 1971).

# Feedback task 12

**LEVEL**

**Intermediate and above**

**AIM**

To look at the patterns of interaction within a group.

**PREPARATION**

Brief the observers.

**PROCEDURE**

**1** Divide the students into groups of five and nominate one student in each group as the observer. The observer should then take a piece of paper and draw circles to represent each of the other members of the group, e.g.

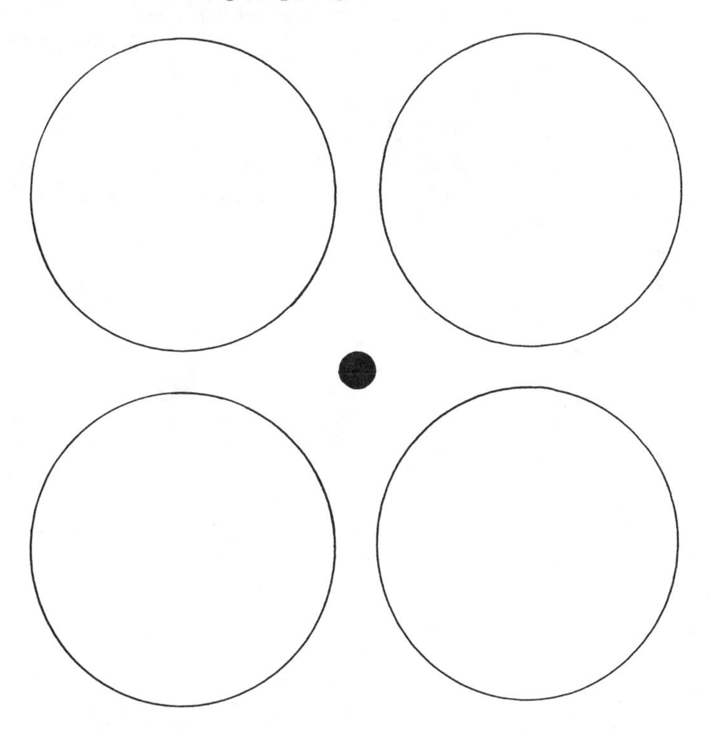

He or she should then write the name of one of the members of the group in each circle.

**2** The students should then be given a discussion task or problem solving task to complete which should potentially involve as much interaction between different members of the group as possible.

Each time somebody speaks the observer should draw an arrow on his sheet from the name of the speaker in the direction of the name of the person the speaker is addressing. If he or she is speaking to the group in general, the observer should draw an arrow pointing *away from the group*.

As each person starts speaking the observer should begin to count to five and then draw the arrow as indicated. The observer should then begin counting again if the same speaker is continuing and draw another arrow. This will help to discriminate between those who speak continuously and those who speak briefly.

Using the information gathered by the observer the group should:

**a.** list in order who spoke the most down to who spoke the least;
**b.** list who spoke the most to whom down to who spoke the least to whom. This should include speaking to the group as a whole.

On the basis of the information listed the group should hold a discussion of the following points:

**a.** Why were the lines of communication as they were?
**b.** Were the lines of communication effective for completing the task, and if not, why not?
**c.** Was everyone happy with the way they participated?
**d.** What things do you think the group should pay attention to in the future?

**Acknowledgement**
This is taken from an idea by Virginia Samuda and Anthony Bruton in *$L_2$ Gas Applied Linguistics Project*, University of Lancaster.

# Bibliography

## Background reading


**Gillian Brown** *Listening to Spoken English*. London: Longman, 1977.

**Gillian Brown and George Yule** *Teaching the Spoken Language*. Cambridge: Cambridge University Press, 1983.

**J. Coates** 'Language and sexism' in a report from the Committee for Linguistics in Education.

**Malcolm Coulthard, David Brazil and Catherine Johns** *Discourse Intonation and Language Teaching*. London: Longman, 1980.

**Malcolm Coulthard** *An Introduction to Discourse Analysis*. London: Longman, 1977.

**David Crystal and Derek Davy** *Advanced Conversational English*. London: Longman, 1975.

**H. P. Grice** 'Logic and conversation' in P. Cole and J. Morgan (eds.) *Syntax and Semantics Volume 3: Speech Acts*. New York: Academic Press, 1975.

**J. J. Gumperz** 'Sociocultural knowledge in conversational inference' in M. Saville-Troike (ed.) *Georgetown University Round Table on Languages and Linguistics*. Washington D.C.: Georgetown University Press, 1977.

**E. T. Hall** *The Silent Language*. New York: Doubleday-Anchor, 1959.

**William Littlewood** *Communicative Language Teaching*. Cambridge: Cambridge University Press, 1981.

**H. Sacks, E. A. Schegloff and G. Jefferson** 'A simplest systematics for the organization of turn-taking for conversation.' *Language* 50/4, 1974.

**Richard W. Schmidt and Jack C. Richards** 'Speech acts and second language learning.' *Applied Linguistics*, Vol. I, No. 2, 1980.

**Henry Widdowson** *Teaching Language as Communication*. Oxford: Oxford University Press, 1978.

## Assessment

**B. Carroll** — *Testing Communicative Performance*. Oxford: Pergamon Press, 1982.

**Keith Morrow** — 'Communicative Language Testing: Revolution or Evolution?' in C. J. Brumfit and K. Johnson (eds.). *The Communicative Approach to Language Teaching*. Oxford: Oxford University Press, 1979.

## Ideas for warmers and controlled activities

**Donna Brandes and Howard Phillips** — *Gamesters' Handbook: 140 Games for Teachers and Group Leaders*. London: Hutchinson, 1979.

**Alan Maley and Alan Duff** — *Drama Techniques in Language Teaching*. Cambridge: Cambridge University Press, 1978 (new edition 1983).

**Gertrude Moskowitz** — *Caring and Sharing in the Foreign Language Class*. Rowley, Mass.: Newbury House, 1978.

**Jane Revell** — *Teaching Techniques for Communicative English*. London: Macmillan, 1979.

**Mario Rinvolucri** — *Grammar Games*. Cambridge: Cambridge University Press, 1985.

**Mario Rinvolucri and Christine Frank** — *Grammar in Action*. Oxford: Pergamon Press, 1983.

## Sources of useful listening material

**Alan Maley and Alan Duff** — *Variations on a Theme*. Cambridge: Cambridge University Press, 1978.

**Rob Nolasco** — *Listening* (Elementary), Oxford Supplementary Skills series. Oxford: Oxford University Press, 1987.

**Mary Underwood** — *What a Story!* Oxford: Oxford University Press, 1976.

**Mary Underwood** — *Have You Heard . . .?* Oxford: Oxford University Press, 1979.

## Ideas for pronunciation teaching

**Ann Baker** — *Tree or Three?* Cambridge: Cambridge University Press, 1982.

**Ann Baker** — *Ship or Sheep?* Cambridge: Cambridge University Press, 1977 (new edition 1981).

**Ann Baker** *Introducing English Pronunciation* (a Teacher's Guide to *Tree or Three?* and *Ship or Sheep?*). Cambridge: Cambridge University Press, 1977.

**G. Broughton *et al*** *Teaching English as a Foreign Language*. London: Routledge & Kegan Paul, 1978.

**Roger Gower and Steve Walters** *Teaching Practice Handbook*. London: Heinemann, 1983.

**B. Haycraft** *The Teaching of Pronunciation*. London: Longman, 1971.

**Peter Hubbard, Hywel Jones, Barbara Thornton and Rod Wheeler** *A Training Course for TEFL*. Oxford: Oxford University Press, 1983.

**Colin Mortimer** *Elements of Pronunciation*. Cambridge: Cambridge University Press, 1976.

**Michael Swan** *Practical English Usage*. Oxford: Oxford University Press, 1980.

**John Trim** *English Pronunciation Illustrated*. Cambridge: Cambridge University Press, 1965.

## Sources of fluency activities

**Christine Frank, Mario Rinvolucri and Marge Berer** *Challenge to Think*. Oxford: Oxford University Press, 1982.

**Friederike Klippel** *Keep Talking*. Cambridge: Cambridge University Press, 1984.

**John Morgan and Mario Rinvolucri** *Once Upon a Time*. Cambridge: Cambridge University Press, 1983.

**Rob Nolasco** *Speaking* (Elementary), Oxford Supplementary Skills series. Oxford: Oxford University Press, 1987.

See also books by Maley & Duff, Moskowitz, and Brandes & Phillips (op. cit.).

## Material on working in groups

**M. L. J. Abercrombie** *Aims and Techniques in Group Teaching*. Society for Research into Higher Education (S.R.H.E.), Report no. 2, 1970.

**D. Barnes** *From Communication to Curriculum*. London: Penguin, 1976.

**E. Berne** *Games People Play*. London: Penguin, 1964.

**P. Buckley, V. Samuda and A. Bruton** 'Sensitizing the learner to group work' in *Practical Papers in English Language Education*, Vol. I. Institute of English Language Education, University of Lancaster.

**Gillian Porter Ladousse** *Role Play*, Resource Books for Teachers series. Oxford: Oxford University Press, 1987.

**Neil Rackham** *Developing Interactive Skills*. Northampton: Wellens Publishing, 1971.

## Introductions to Community Language Learning

**Rod Bolitho** 'But where's the teacher?' in *Practical English Teaching*, March 1983.

**E. W. Stevick** *Memory, Meaning and Method*. Rowley, Mass.: Newbury House, 1976.

**E. W. Stevick** *Teaching Languages – A Way and Ways*. Rowley, Mass.: Newbury House, 1980.